Handbooks for the English Classroom

Assessment

Michael Harris and Paul McCann

HEINEMANN ENGLISH LANGUAGE TEACHING
A division of Heinemann Publishers (Oxford) Ltd
Halley Court, Jordan Hill, Oxford OX2 8EJ

OXFORD MADRID ATHENS PARIS FLORENCE PRAGUE
SÃO PAULO CHICAGO MELBOURNE AUCKLAND SINGAPORE TOKYO
IBADAN GABORONE JOHANNESBURG PORTSMOUTH (NH)

ISBN 0 435 28252 2

©Michael Harris, Paul McCann 1994

First published 1994

Designed by Mike Brain

Cover illustration by Jacky Rough

Illustrated by:
Nick Hardcastle
Geoff Jones

The authors would like to thank Pauline Rea-Dickens, Alex Teasdale and Annie McDonald for helpful suggestions, Christina and Maria José for support and patience.

Printed and bound in Scotland by Thomson Litho Ltd.
94 95 96 97 98 99 9 8 7 6 5 4 3 2 1

CONTENTS

Introduction   2

Prejudices and problems   2

Suggestions and solutions   3

Chapter 1   Informal assessment   5
1.1   Introduction   5
1.2   When and what to assess   7
1.3   Informal assessment of linguistic factors   9
1.4   Informal assessment of non-linguistic factors   21
1.5   Results from informal assessment   24
             Action points   25

Chapter 2   Formal assessment   26
2.1   Why test?   26
2.2   Planning assessment programmes   30
2.3   Choosing test formats   34
2.4   Writing, administering and marking tests   49
2.5   Results from formal assessment   60
             Suggested answers   61
             Action points   62

Chapter 3   Self-assessment   63
3.1   Introduction   63
3.2   Laying the foundations   68
3.3   Assessing performance   74
3.4   Reviewing progress   80
3.5   Results from self-assessment   86
             Suggested answers   88
             Action points   88

Glossary of terms   89

Bibliography   94

INTRODUCTION

What is assessment?

This handbook deals with *assessment*. It is very important to make a clear distinction between *assessment* and *evaluation*. As teachers, when we carry out *assessment*, we have to measure the performance of our students and the progress they make. We also need to diagnose the problems they have and provide our learners with useful feedback. *Evaluation* on the other hand involves looking at *all* the factors that influence the learning process, such as syllabus objectives, course design, materials, methodology, teacher performance and assessment. Assessment and evaluation are often linked, because assessment is one of the most valuable sources of information about what is happening in a learning environment.

Prejudices and problems

Assessment is generally seen as something done to students by teachers. Many students may feel panic and confusion. Tests descend upon them from time to time and have to be 'got through'. The more able ones may even enjoy these experiences, as they can assert their superiority over the rest of the class. However, many students feel anxious, worried and inadequate. There is often great pressure on them to succeed and if they do not, they become branded as failures. Unfortunately this competition creates more losers than winners. Many teachers feel little better. Some feel that tests are only useful as a way of motivating students to work harder and virtually all of us feel insecure and uncomfortable when we have to pass or fail students.

Many of these negative attitudes towards assessment come from the generalised feeling of a divorce between learning and teaching on the one hand, and assessment on the other. The fundamental reason for this is that assessment often does not feed back into the learning and teaching process.

◆ Firstly, assessment is often seen as synonymous with testing. Testing or *formal assessment*, where test or exam conditions are established, is certainly an important way of assessing learners. However, it is not the only one and both informal assessment and self-assessment are vital. *Informal assessment* is assessment carried out by the teacher not under special test conditions, but in the normal classroom environment (for example with students helping each other when necessary). *Self assessment* is that carried out by students themselves of their own progress and problems.

◆ Secondly, assessment is seen as something that happens after learning has finished, rather than during the learning process. Tests or exams are often given at the end of term or of a course and they are often regarded as a rather painful but necessary prelude to the holidays. For many learners the information that this assessment gives them about their performance and progress comes much too late to be *formative*, to feed into their own learning.

◆ Another problem is the kind of feedback that learners are given. Often information about how well learners are doing is expressed only by a grade or mark. The grade classifies students, but does not give any real help by telling students what their specific problems are and by making suggestions to overcome them.

◆ An additional drawback of the way assessment is carried out in many classrooms is that it often concentrates on only one part of what has gone on in the classroom. It is easier to test tangible knowledge of grammar for example, than to assess performance at say speaking. An over-reliance on grammar tests gives students the clear message that they have been wasting their time trying to communicate in class. What matters is grammar.

◆ Yet another reason for negative attitudes to assessment among students is that, rather than give them the opportunity to show what they have learnt, it tries to catch students out, to reveal what they have not learnt. Learners also feel alienated by assessment because they have no role in it, apart from as passive participants. For many learners in this situation, assessment must seem arbitrary and at times even unfair. Sometimes they get on with their teacher, sometimes they do not. Sometimes they are lucky and revise the right material for a test, sometimes they are unlucky.

On the other hand, surprisingly little help is given to teachers to assess effectively and fairly, to carry out assessment that reflects what has gone on in the classroom. The result is that as teachers we are often on the defensive when dealing with learners, parents and school administrators.

An added problem is often that of the effect of public examinations, both national and international. Not only is the stress factor for learners greatly increased, but the examinations can have a profound *washback effect* (*the influence of assessment on both teaching and learning*). In some cases examinations can dominate what goes on in language classrooms for the months and even years leading up to them. If all these exams were forward-thinking and communicative this would be positive. Unfortunately this is not always the case.

Suggestions and solutions

What model of assessment can be offered as an alternative to this gloomy picture? Let us look briefly at three of the basic questions that this book will try to answer: *'When, who and how should we assess?'*

When should we assess?

To provide constant feedback which itself helps to direct the learning process, assessment has got to be a continuous process going on at different levels. At an everyday level it is important for some kind of informal assessment by the teacher to be done in nearly every lesson, hand in hand with learning. More in-depth formal assessment should then be done at frequent points throughout the course, giving feedback to both the learner and the teacher (rather than waiting for the end of term). It is important for this to be integrated into the course, not only reflecting course content, but in many cases developing and extending topic areas covered. At the same time self-assessment needs to be done at regular intervals, so that learners can be given an opportunity to think about what progress they are making and what their problems are. At the end of a course all the assessment that has gone on should then be put together and final decisions about students' progress made.

Who should assess?

Assessment has traditionally been the exclusive domain of the teacher. Without doubt we should not abdicate this responsibility for assessing classwork and homework informally and for setting and marking tests that are done under formal conditions. However, it is possible to complement and improve our judgements by asking students to participate in the process themselves.

Not only do we gather useful information through self-assessment, but involvement of students in the assessment process also means that their attitudes towards their own learning can change significantly. Rather than being motivated by the threat of examinations, students can start to feel more responsible for their own progress, thus acquiring greater and more intrinsic motivation for learning. At the same time, self-assessment can help students to become more efficient as learners, to diagnose their own weaknesses and problems and then to try to do something about them.

Self-assessment is a relatively new concept. However, as we will see in *Chapter 3*, involving learners in this aspect of our jobs does not threaten our position. On the contrary, it helps us by giving us more information as well as by training learners to think for themselves.

Finally, in addition to enlisting the help and participation of our learners in assessment, we should work with as many colleagues as possible rather than working on our own. A co-operative approach saves both time and work, and pools vital knowledge and resources.

How should we assess?

Assessment must be done *constructively*, focusing on achievement rather than on failure. It should allow students to demonstrate what they know, rather than trying to catch them out. As classroom teachers we are assessing our learners' progress and most of our students should be able to pass. If this is not the case, we have to take another look at what has gone on during the course.

Assessment must also have some degree of *reliability* ie that it is consistent and that under the same conditions and with the same performance by students our assessment produces the same or at least similar results. If we do not establish clear criteria and work out clear procedures for assessing beforehand and try to keep to them, there is a danger that we will discriminate against some students. We should also inform students of at least the basic outlines of our assessment, so that not only is our assessment reliable, but it is seen to be reliable and fair by our students.

It is also very important to be clear about what we want to assess and to ensure that we are assessing that and not something else, that our assessment has *validity*. For example, if we want to assess listening we must only consider understanding and not assess our students' ability to read or write or their ability to produce accurate language. To reach the goal of *validity* in our assessment it is thus very important that we have clear assessment objectives in the first place and then try to make sure that these objectives are reached.

Another important feature is *practicality*. Any approach to assessment must not be too time-consuming, in terms of class hours and of our own time outside the class. Assessment is only one aspect of our jobs and cannot be allowed to detract from teaching or preparation time. It should also be practical in terms of physical resources such as tape-recorders and photocopies.

A final element is *accountability*. As professionals, teachers should be able to provide learners, parents, institutions and society in general, with clear indications of what progress has been made and if it has not, why that is so. We should be able to explain the rationale behind the way assessment takes place and how conclusions are drawn, rather than hiding behind a smoke screen of professional secrecy.

In the following pages of this handbook we aim to discuss some of the issues in assessment, to look at some of the options open to us as classroom teachers and to provide practical ideas for teachers to try out in the classroom.

◆ First, we will look at *informal assessment* done by the teacher.
◆ Then we will examine *formal assessment* or 'testing', which provides us with additional information about our students.
◆ Finally, we will consider assessment done by the students themselves, *self-assessment*.

At the end of each chapter we will think about how to deal with results from each form of assessment.

1 Informal assessment

1.1 Introduction

The first of the three chapters in this book will look at informal assessment in and outside the classroom. We will look at when and how to carry out this kind of assessment of both linguistic and non-linguistic factors (like attitude). Finally we will look at what to do with the results from this kind of assessment.

Informal assessment is:

Informal assessment is a way of collecting information about our students' performance in normal classroom conditions. This is done without establishing test conditions such as in the case of formal assessment. Informal assessment is sometimes referred to as continuous assessment as it is done over a period of time like a term or an academic year. However, formal assessment can also be done continuously as we will see in the next chapter.

When we are in the classroom with our students we intuitively assess their performance when speaking, writing, reading or listening. We can see which students are performing well and which students are finding difficulties. We are also aware of students' attitudes, how much effort they are making and how much they are participating in class activities. However, to carry out effective informal assessment we need to carry out systematic observation.
- Firstly we need to work out what we are going to assess, as it is obviously impossible to assess all students' performance all the time.
- Then we must establish clear criteria for assessing students and not only rely on rough impressions.
- Finally it is important to link the informal assessment we do with our formal assessment (tests) and with self-assessment done by the students themselves.

The information we give students should help them identify areas which may cause them difficulties when they do formal tests. We must also give our students feedback and help them to think for themselves about the information, as well as heightening their awareness of how they assess themselves.

Informal assessment is not:

- *Informal assessment* is not a replacement for other forms of assessment such as formal or self-assessment and should not be considered as the only way of obtaining and giving information about our students.
- It is not a way of avoiding tests altogether which allows the teacher to make decisions about students based purely on informal observation.
- It is not a form of assessment without criteria on which to make judgements about students' progress.
- It is not a single system which can be used by all teachers in all contexts in all schools or teaching establishments – each teacher or group of teachers need(s) to find a system which is suitable to their particular situation.
- It is not a form of assessment to be considered in isolation from other forms of assessment but rather as part of a larger, overall programme which should be a balanced system of decision-making.

Informal assessment – Part of a system

Work with a colleague or colleagues.

Look at the statements below about assessment.

Discuss each statement and then assign a grade for each statement in the following way:

> **5** Agree strongly
> **4** Agree
> **3** Indifferent
> **2** Disagree
> **1** Disagree strongly

1 Informal assessment of language skills is the most important area for us to assess informally.
   5   4   3   2   1

2 Non-linguistic factors should not be assessed – this is the job of psychologists.
   5   4   3   2   1

3 Informal assessment is simply the systematic observation of our students.
   5   4   3   2   1

4 Informal assessment could replace all those time-consuming tests that I have to give.
   5   4   3   2   1

5 Informal assessment should be part of an overall system of assessment.
   5   4   3   2   1

6 Informal assessment means what it says : 'informal' – I observe and make a judgement based on my experience – rating scales are a waste of time.
   5   4   3   2   1

7 An adequate system of informal assessment already exists in my school – we take in essays and compositions and mark them.
   5   4   3   2   1

8 Informal assessment can only take place in the classroom.
   5   4   3   2   1

9 Even without set criteria, I always mark written work in the same way – I know what I am looking for.
   5   4   3   2   1

10 Students sometimes act differently when I walk round the class and listen to their conversations.
    5   4   3   2   1

1.2 When and what to assess

Traditionally, we tend to think of this type of assessment as consisting solely of 'marking an essay' done for homework or the teacher walking round the class during an activity to get a vague idea of whether the students 'are doing all right' or not. The classroom is obviously the most important place to assess students informally. It is also where most data is available. Students spend more time here than in any other learning environment and here we can monitor students' performance in all four skills – speaking, listening, reading and writing. However we can also assess work outside the classroom, eg looking at samples of students' work or collecting in workbooks and vocabulary books.

One of the first things we need to do is to work out how much we are going to assess as there are many other aspects of our job that require attention both in and outside the classroom. In the classroom we need to think about classroom management and reaching the aims of the lesson first. The time we have for assessment is limited. Similarly, outside the classroom we have lots of other things to do like planning and materials creation. We must make sure that marking does not take up all our time. Because of all these pressures, it is useful to think about what things we are going to assess consciously and which things we are just going to get an impression of.

Think about how you carry out informal assessment with your students. Look at the list of items below. Either on your own or with a colleague or colleagues, decide which of the items you assess informally by giving a mark and which you merely get an impression of.

Linguistic factors	I get an overall impression	I give a specific mark
a written homework		
b written grammar activities		
c speaking activities		
d projects		
e listening tasks		
f reading tasks		
g writing tasks		
h vocabulary activities		
Non-linguistic factors		
a attitude/effort		
b participation in class		
c group work		
d organisation of work		
e presentation of work		
f punctuality		

Are there any other factors that you consider?

In addition to thinking about what to assess it can be useful to think about the *weighting* that you are going to give each area. We will look at this in more detail when we look at planning assessment programmes in the next chapter. However, it is worth thinking about your priorities at this stage; which areas you are going to give most marks for. The priorities that you have will be those outlined in the syllabus plan of the school that you work in, but it is worth establishing clearly the *weighting* in your informal assessment at the beginning of a year. To decide what is a pass or a fail you need to balance the four skills, language and non-linguistic factors. For example you may want to weight the final assessment in favour of speaking or listening if you have spent proportionately more class time on these skills. In this case you should give a higher percentage of the overall score to these areas and less for other areas like language and writing.

Another key consideration is how much informal assessment you are going to do compared with formal assessment or testing. If there are a lot of tests during the term or year, then informal assessment on a large scale may not be adding much to the information gained about a student. However if there are very few tests, informal assessment may take on a more important and influential role and may contribute more information than in the previous case. Everything depends on specific institutions and the way each institution works will affect the exact weighting of each area of assessment.

If you have freedom to decide yourself on the balance between informal and formal assessment in your classroom, it is worth thinking about it before starting off a course. It is also important to inform your students so that they have a clear idea about how they are going to be assessed.

> ## Weighting: informal/formal assessment
>
> What is an ideal balance for your classes between informal assessment and formal assessment or tests?
> Which of these comments reflects your classroom situation?
>
> - '*I do nearly all my assessment informally. I have small classes of about fifteen to twenty students and we have quite a few hours of English a week. I suppose that I get 80% of my marks from informal assessment and 20% from tests.*'
>
> - '*I have about twenty-five or thirty students in my classes and we only have three hours of English a week. I get 50% of my marks from informal assessment: the work they do in class, projects and homework. The other 50% I get from short tests which I give throughout the term.*'
>
> - '*I do nearly all of my assessment formally, through tests. I get some marks from work that students do in class and I always give them an oral mark. However I have over forty in each class and we only have two hours of English each week. Because of this I have to get most of my marks from short tests which I give during the term. I suppose that I get 70% of my marks from tests and 30% from informal assessment.*'

1.3 Informal assessment of linguistic factors

The most common way of assessing students informally has traditionally been by marking pieces of work that students do either in class or for homework. These marks are then added up at the end of the assessment period to work out a final grade. Without doubt this marking of students' work is one of the most important sources of information that we have. However, this approach has serious drawbacks:

◆ Firstly, it means that we might tend to concentrate on written work and on grammar exercises rather than focusing on oral skills.
◆ Secondly, when we mark work we might assign marks on the basis of the 'impression' that we have of the work. We are not thinking in detail about what exactly we expect the students to achieve.
◆ Finally, when we add up marks at the end of term we tend to make judgements in terms of impressions and without a clear idea of what we are assessing.

Therefore, it is important to make a conscious effort to assess oral skills during classes and establish clear criteria to help us assess specific performance by students and come to decisions about students' progress.

Assessment criteria can be described in terms of what we expect our students to be able to do. This may be *Yes/No* or *Pass/Fail* ie the student can or cannot satisfy a certain criterion. An example may be 'ability to work within a group'. With linguistic factors, however, it is much more likely that students can satisfy criteria to a greater or lesser degree ie they will be improving along a continuum on which at the present moment they are quite good at something and with more practice they will become better, eg oral expression.

In these cases a more descriptive system of grading is needed than *Yes/No* or *Pass/Fail*. An alternative is to grade student performance in these areas into a number of *bands,* eg *0* is a poor performance and *5* is an excellent performance. We can then describe each level or *band*. The more bands we have the more delicate and descriptive the system will be. At the same time, the more delicate and descriptive the system is, the finer the distinctions you will have to identify in student performances. This may prove to be more difficult than it sounds – assigning a student a *13* instead of a *14* on a *20* band scale may prove to be a very difficult task due to the fine distinctions between the two bands. On the other hand, the fewer the bands we have, the easier the task is to assign band numbers to students as the distinction between a *3* and a *4* on a *5* band scale will be greater than on a *10* band scale and will therefore be more easily identified. Of course, the fewer the bands, the more rough and ready the system is.

Bearing all this in mind, what we need is to find the optimum number of bands with clear and easily understandable band descripters for our purpose. If we find this, then we will have a system which is usable and suited to our needs.

We will now look in more detail at assessment of the fours skills, of language and assessment of non-linguistic factors.

Speaking

Informal assessment is particularly important for speaking as many teachers have practical difficulties in organising oral tests (lack of a place to do them or lack of time). Because of this, oral assessment in many situations has to be done informally. In addition, informal assessment of speaking can have an important effect on learners. If they see that speaking English and participating in class is rewarded they will be more motivated to participate actively and try to use English in the class.

Informal assessment of speaking is done by observing students' oral performance in class, by monitoring speaking activities as they happen. In a busy classroom when you have lots of other things to do this is not always easy. If you are walking around the class monitoring a class oral activity (for example all students are working in small groups discussing a particular issue or solving a problem) you may well obtain a fairly good idea of class performance as a whole and individual performance in particular areas. You might come to the conclusion that a particular class needs remedial work in pronunciation, or that a particular student's intonation is not as acceptable as that of other members of the same class.

As you will probably spend a lot of time with your classes you will gain many insights into these areas as a rapport builds up between you and the students and you begin to function as one working unit with mutual confidence. It must be pointed out here that your intuitive judgements are often very useful. One way in which you can systematise this gathering of impressions is by giving students points based on pre-defined criteria when you see that they are performing well, either in groups or in front of the whole class. At the end of the assessment period you can then add up the points that students have to get an idea of how well they are doing.

However, the question of unreliability and inaccuracy of judgement should be considered in the following ways. Firstly we may get a distorted view of overall class ability if we cannot listen to all students during all activities as so often happens with large numbers of students. Secondly, we may get a distorted view of particular students who might try harder when they know we are listening to them; on the other hand, students may perform worse in the knowledge that the teacher is actively monitoring them.

The first thing we need to do is to produce a system which attempts to give us the possibility of making reliable and objective judgements about our students. The criteria we choose and the descriptors for each criteria, eg on a 5 band scale will provide a degree of reliability we would not have if we used no criteria at all except our intuition. The criteria might focus on a particular aspect of speaking, eg fluency, intonation, pronunciation, self-correction where necessary etc. What our criteria will do for us is allow us to place a student on a scale according to his/her performance at any one given moment in time.

We can establish our own criteria, but if other teachers in the school are using different criteria there can be a considerable amount of unreliability in assessment in the school. Therefore it is important firstly to agree on criteria for assessing students with our colleagues. The following step is to make sure that we all agree on exactly what the assessment scales mean. This standardisation of perceptions can be achieved through meetings, discussions and where possible listening to recorded performances and using these for standardisation purposes.

Our bands may have more than one aspect of speaking and may describe the speaking skill as one or two general criteria. Look at the following band scale:

> **5** Speaks fluently – almost no errors
> **4** Speaks quite fluently – some errors
> **3** Some difficulty in speaking – many errors
> **2** Difficulty with speaking – almost incomprehensible
> **1** Unable to use language – incomprehensible

While this scale may serve as a rough guide to the fluency and number of errors our students are making and while it may be possible to place our students on this scale as a result of informal observation, there are certain questions and problems we would have to clear up before using it; *What does 'fluently' actually mean? What or how much is 'some' in band scale 4? Do the bands move from one to the other in a uniform way or is there a big jump between one particular band scale and another?* and most importantly – *Is this exactly what we want to assess?*

Oral assessment criteria

Look at the scale on page 10 and, if at all possible with your colleagues, write a fuller description of the bands. Think about including descriptions of these things:

- fluency (speed/amount of hesitation)
- message (relevance and appropriacy)
- accuracy (grammatical and lexical errors)
- pronunciation (sounds/intonation/stress)

Compare your descriptions with those on page 44

Once you and your colleagues have decided on the assessment criteria and the type of scale to use, you will want to put the system into practice. How can you implement the system? What follows is a list of suggested ways of carrying out systematic observation and recording the results. However, you should adapt these methods to your own particular situation and where necessary think of other ways of systematically observing and recording your findings which may be more suited to your needs. No single method is suitable in all teaching situations or all institutions.

- ◆ The first step is to produce band scales to assess oral performance. You can either do this on your own or (much better) work them out with your colleagues. Having done this you can then use them to assess your student's competence at any given time, eg at the end of each month or at the end of each term. Your judgements will be based on your observation of students in the preceding period. It is also possible to give your students the same bands and ask them to assess themselves. Your assessment and that done by learners can then be compared. Furthermore, assessment criteria should be made available to everybody concerned including institutions and parents of students. (*For further discussion, see self-assessment page 63*).
- ◆ Another alternative is to assess students' performance at a particular time. The best way of doing this is perhaps to tell students that you will be assessing them over the next few lessons. Then you can make sure that in the lessons there are a series of speaking tasks. With large classes it is probably a good idea to choose five or six students to assess in each lesson (though do not tell them as when they know they have been assessed they may stop making an effort!). During the tasks you can go around the class and write down your assessments of students' performance. The best tasks to use are those that students normally do in class and in general group or pairwork activities are the most suitable: pairwork interviews, group surveys, roleplays, information gap activities etc. You can though use some whole class activities, where students give a presentation (individually or in groups) or where they act out roleplays that they have prepared.

Both of these activities can be a good conclusion to project and task based work and also provide good opportunities for peer and self-assessment with assessment bands given to the students. The first method suggested measures potential performance this method measures actual performance in tasks. As well as assessing speaking by oral bands alone, they can be used in conjunction with a set of pre-defined criteria which are objectives to be aimed at and which are *Yes/No* type criteria, eg *'participates in discussions'*. They can also be used along with more systematic impression marking, for example giving students points for good performance throughout the term.

◆ The last question to ask is *'When we should carry out informal assessment of speaking?'* This will depend on the time which is available and the number of hours of class you have each week. It is obvious that the more hours you have in the classroom with the students, the greater the opportunity to assess. Another factor to consider is the frequency with which you have to give reports on your students. If results of assessments are to be reported each term, then the informal assessment programme will have to take this into account and will have to tie in with the other forms of assessment being used to make up the overall assessment of each student. If results are to be reported each academic year, the informal assessment programme will have to take this into account in the same way.

Writing

Assessing our students' written work can be very time consuming and unless you are careful you can find yourself with many hours of marking, which takes time away from other aspects of teaching like lesson planning. It is thus very important to choose the most important pieces of writing that students do and not try to assess every piece of written work. Thus we need to decide how many and what sort of compositions we are going to assess. Younger secondary learners may not need to do as much writing as older secondary students who have to do writing in public examinations. The degree of importance that writing has should be reflected in your syllabus plans. Another point to consider is the amount of writing which should be done individually and that which is done in groups. Group writing activities are not only good for developing writing skills, particularly in a mixed ability situation, they can also make your marking load more viable and enable you to give more feedback to more of your students. For example, in a large class of over forty it is more practical to mark ten group compositions every week than forty individual ones.

Another point to consider is giving feedback. We need to make very sure that the feedback we give to students is used by them. It can be very frustrating to spend a lot of time marking when students just look at the mark and nothing else. When we give feedback to our students it is important that they think about it themselves and work out how they can do better in the future. Therefore the link between informal assessment of writing and self-assessment is vital.

Another crucial factor is the need to make sure that the assessment we do of our students is as reliable as possible. For example, if you are correcting or assessing an essay or composition, you will often give an 'impression' or 'impressionistic mark'. This means that you will read through the piece of work once, twice or perhaps more times, and give it a mark. This could be some point on a scale of *1–10* or a letter from *A– E*. The chances are that if you are assessing the work from a class like this you will apply some sort of criteria which you may have in your head, without consciously listing them. Even if you are working on your own it would probably be much better if you actually listed these criteria, and it would certainly be very useful for students to know exactly what they are.

However, we need to think about the question of unreliability and inaccuracy of judgement in several ways. Firstly, when we are marking by impression it may happen that we give a different mark to the same piece of work on a different day or even part of a day. For example, when we are tired at the end of the day we could give a composition a lower mark than in the morning. Conversely we might be more generous on a Friday than on a Monday. Secondly, as we are all different we might have different sets of criteria. Thus a student could get a different mark for the same piece of work if it were marked by different teachers.

As with speaking we need to think very carefully about what criteria we use.

Look at the following scale:

> **5** Excellent writer
> **4** Good writer
> **3** Modest writer
> **2** Marginal writer
> **1** Poor writer

If we use this scale, we need to define previously what the meaning of the descriptors is.

For example:
What makes a student an 'excellent' writer rather than a 'good' writer?
◆ Is it comprehensibility?
◆ Is it grammatical accuracy?
◆ Is it spelling?
◆ Is it the way they organise the text?

When we are working out rating scales and descriptors to use there are two possibilities. We can either produce overall descriptions of writing ability or concentrate on different aspects of writing and separate these aspects out into individual scales. General overall descriptions, ie those containing different features of ability, are called *holistic* scales. Those which separate out different aspects of ability are called *analytic* scales.

Example of holistic scale for writing ability:

> **5** Constructs grammatically correct sentences and phrases and shows full mastery of appropriate vocabulary. Text is organised coherently. Correct spelling at all times. Excellent content and presentation. Message wholly relevant
> **4** In general, grammatically correct sentences and phrases but some errors which do not affect understanding. Does not use appropriate vocabulary at all times. Some difficulties with organisation of text. Some errors in spelling. Good content and presentation. Message mostly relevant.
> **3** Grammatical errors and use of vocabulary affects understanding as does organisation of text. Many errors in spelling. Satisfactory content and presentation. Message not always relevant.
> **2** Text understood with difficulty due to inaccurate grammar and inappropriate use of vocabulary. Poor content and presentation. Message generally lacks relevancy.
> **1** Impossible to understand text due to frequency of grammatical errors and incoherence of organisation. Poor spelling Message irrelevant.

Informal assessment – Number of bands

Look at the 1– 5 band scale in the box below.
Work alone or with a colleague or colleagues and expand the five bands into a ten band scale by writing more detailed descriptions.

5 Constructs grammatically correct sentences and phrases and shows full mastery of appropriate vocabulary.
  Text is organised coherently and is well structured.
  Correct spelling at all times.
4 In general, grammatically correct sentences and phrases but some errors which do not affect understanding.
  Does not use appropriate vocabulary at all times.
  Some difficulties with organisation of text.
  Some errors in spelling.
3 Grammatical errors and use of vocabulary affects understanding as does organisation of text. Many errors in spelling.
2 Text understood with difficulty due to inaccurate grammar and inappropriate use of vocabulary.
1 Impossible to understand text due to frequency of grammatical errors and incoherence of organisation. Poor spelling.

When you have finished, answer the following questions:
• What difficulties did you encounter when writing the expanded scale?
• Do you think that with your expanded scale teachers would find it easy to differentiate between a *6* and a *7* or a *3* and a *4*?
• Does each activity, (eg spelling) appear in each band?
• Do you think that your *holistic* band scale could or should be broken up into analytic scales?
• By looking at your ten point scale, would it be obvious what is an acceptable level, ie the cut-off point or 'pass mark'?

Analytic scales separate the aspects or activities given in the box above and thus cater for the student who cuts across the bands and their descriptors. For example, it is possible that a student may be a *3* in the scale above for grammatical accuracy but a *2* for spelling. However, both *analytic* and *holistic* scales can be used successfully to assess ability if the descriptors are clear enough and if perceptions are standardised. If a student falls into more than one band on a holistic scale, the teacher should be able to choose the most appropriate or best fit for that student's work.

When marking students' compositions you may find that rather than trying to measure performance comprehensively, you can focus on a couple of aspects. For example, when assessing a story you could focus on text organisation and linking, not marking grammatical accuracy or spelling. For a project poster giving information about a country you could focus on content and presentation. While this approach does not measure all aspects of writing it is a good way of giving students manageable feedback.

Whatever set of criteria you use it is important to tell students what they are beforehand so they will be aware of what is expected of them and will hopefully think more closely about your assessment when they receive it. The clear establishment of criteria enables them to assess their own work as we will see in the chapter on self-assessment. Another thing to consider is how you are actually going to give feedback to your students. If you correct everything and write the corrections on their work students can be very de-motivated. There is nothing worse than receiving a piece of work back which is covered with red ink! One way in which you can do this and at the same time get students to think about their mistakes is by using a correction code. Through a code you can signal problems that students are having. When you give work back students can work either individually or in groups to see if they can correct their own work. While they are doing this you can go around the class and answer any problems that they might have.

Correction codes

Look at this correction code. Work out your own code to use with your students.

S spelling   **V** vocabulary
P punctuation   **G** grammar
WO word order   **Pa** paragraphs
L linking   **Pr** prepositions

When you use a code with your students, go over it on the board and to explain give them examples of mistakes and problems.

When you make judgements about your learners' progress in writing over a period of time you can add up the results that they have had in their compositions or use the work they have done to assess them globally, using the rating scales looked at earlier here. An important point to remember is that if you have been doing a lot of group and project work it will be necessary to complement this with some formal assessment, so that you can check on individual performance.

Listening

We normally develop listening skills in the classroom in *lockstep* fashion. This means that all the students listen to one text at the same time. Most text books or coursebooks include listening passages for use in the classroom. Typical student tasks involve filling in boxes with information, ticking true or false options, ordering events in chronological order and others designed to develop listening skills.

We can informally assess students' listening proficiency by getting an impression of what they have understood or by simply looking at the answers given by any one or more student(s).We can monitor and assess students' listening proficiency whilst monitoring activities such as pair work activities or reactions to instructions from you.

One simple way of checking on answers may be asking for a show of hands to find out how many students, eg answered *10* correctly, *9* correctly, *7*, *6*, *5* and so on. Perhaps there are students who may put up their hand at 8 when they actually answered *3* items correctly – this can give you false results and may also imply an attitude problem on the part of one or more student(s). Extralinguistic clues can often be a basis on which to assess a student's listening proficiency, eg facial gestures, especially eyes – *'I could tell he didn't understand a word because he just looked blank'.* Or the converse situation – *'I could tell she understood everything because she nodded in agreement at everything I said'.* Obviously, neither may be an accurate assessment of these students' proficiency in listening. In the first case the student may have understood more than credited for but was simply not interested. In the second case the student may have understood nothing but wanted to give the opposite impression by nodding.

An alternative would be to go through the answers one by one and ask the class after each question who answered correctly. In this way, those who scored highly are not being overtly praised and those who achieved low scores are not being asked to admit this in front of the rest of the class and are thus not placed in a potentially threatening situation. You should find that this method of eliciting scores will provide more honest and open reporting from students as the element of competition and perceived threat has been removed. You should also make it clear to students why you are asking for information. You can monitor class responses to each question and assess:
♦ the class as a whole in relation to particular questions in the listening task
♦ any students who do not raise their hands very often and who have therefore gained low scores in the task, thereby identifying quickly and efficiently problem areas and students who may be having problems with listening.

Another way of assessing understanding of texts is to ask students to recycle what they have heard. This can be in the form of recycling orally or in written form. For example, following a section of listening text, students can be asked to summarise what they have heard. In large classes, this can be inefficient in terms of time and if individual students are asked in front of the rest of the class it may have a negative effect, by producing a threatening situation for the shy or less able student. A way around this is to ask students to work in groups or pairs and to report to their partners the important points of a text. Alternatively, another way of checking is to refocus the question by saying that you want to know the results in order to establish the difficulty of the task.

A further method of assessment is to use a recorded text as the basis for a speaking activity. For example, a recorded text about the economy of an island may be used as a prologue to a speaking task in which students are asked to discuss the problems of the island and the solutions to them. During the speaking phase you could go around the class and listen to the discussions, focusing on how pairs are using the information that they have been given in the listening text. As well as using listening texts you can assess students ability to understand you or other students in the class. You can gauge ability to understand language by observing student reaction to instructions. Here you will be able to observe those students who may be having problems with listening simply because they are not able to follow your instructions. Also during speaking activities you can go around the class and observe students' ability to understand each other.

You may want or need to make a judgement of listening ability. You can collect marks from listening activities that students have done and that you have taken in. One point to bear in mind here is that listening can be easily tested in this way and that it may not be worth doing the same things twice. When you come to make an overall judgement of listening ability, you can use band scales as for speaking and writing. Once again, you need bands which reflect the kind of listening that you have been doing. For example, the band scale shown on page 17 focuses on aspects such as simple/complex messages, different forms of text presentation (eg radio, TV, song etc.) and differentiation between implicit and explicit information.

Example of band scales for listening ability:

> **5** Can understand complex messages
>   Can understand different oral presentations
>   Can distinguish between explicit and implicit information
> **4** Sometimes has difficulty with some complex messages
>   Can understand most oral presentations
>   In general, can distinguish explicit and implicit information
> **3** Has difficulty with complex messages
>   Has difficulty with some oral presentations
>   Cannot, in general, distinguish between explicit and implicit information
> **2** Cannot understand complex messages
>   Has difficulty with most types of oral presentation
>   Cannot distinguish between explicit and implicit information
> **1** Cannot understand simple messages
>   Cannot understand any type of oral presentation

Choose five or six students from your class.
During a listening activity in normal class hours, use the above rating scale for listening to assess your students' listening ability.

Reading

We often do reading tasks in class in *lockstep* fashion: the whole class reading one text and answering questions on it. Typical examples are the skimming and scanning activities so widely used or the 'comprehension questions' at the end of a text.

There are various ways of assessing this kind of reading in the classroom. The first is by going around the class while students are doing a reading activity and observing which students seem to be understanding it and which are having difficulties. The impressions that you get from this can be misleading as some students will be reluctant to admit difficulties. Another way is by checking class understanding of four or five points from a given reading passage. You can go through the answers with the whole class and afterwards ask for a show of hands of what questions they got right. As mentioned before with listening, this is not a very reliable source of information. An alternative is to collect in answers to reading texts and mark them yourself. Because this is something you can easily do as a test you may prefer to do this kind of activity as part of formal rather than informal assessment.

When assessing reading in this way a factor to bear in mind is subject knowledge. Some students may know a lot about the subject of the text and thus have a clear advantage over those who know little or nothing about it. For example if you are looking at a scientific text non-science based students are at a disadvantage, whereas the science students are considerably helped. In this situation your judgement of these students' ability to read would probably not be very accurate.

Answering a few questions about a text does not give reliable information about overall understanding of it. One solution to the problem is similar to that identified in the section on listening ie recycling. This may take the form of discussion of reading passages or writing about reading texts. For example students can read a letter and then write a reply to it or read a text and then roleplay a situation from it. Jigsaw reading can be useful here, when you divide a text up and different groups have to tell the others about their part of the text. One way of checking understanding is by asking students to tell you about a text in their own language.

Students can also work out their own tasks on texts for other students to do.

By looking at understanding of specific texts we are not really catering for students who have different reading styles, speeds, interests and ability. In mixed ability classes it can be particularly interesting to assess individual reading. Some schools have a library and in these cases you may be able to use it for this kind of reading. If you do not have one, a mini-library could be set up in the classroom. There are commercially available series of graded readers which give clear indications of the number of words used and approximately how many hours of English a student should have studied for in order to be able to cope with the texts in the reader. If you can set up an individual reading scheme you can monitor the activities, talk to individual students, helping out where necessary and thus be able to make judgements about reading ability for different individuals. One-to-one conversation is a key concept here. You may wish to discuss a text, reasons for its choice and its difficulty level with individual students while the class as a whole is performing a task or completing a worksheet. As well as assessment through oral feedback, a quicker way is to get students to write about what they have read.

Informal assessment – Reading records

Look at the Reading Record Form below:

READING RECORD FORM

Name _____

Class _____

Title of book _____

Author _____

Summary of plot

_____

_____

_____

_____

Personal opinion

_____

_____

_____

_____

The reading record form on page 18 would allow you to:
◆ monitor what your students are reading
◆ assess whether they have understood the main points of the text they have read
◆ assess how students have reacted to the text by giving them the opportunity to make a brief criticism
◆ informally assess their written expression

Photocopy the Reading Record Form and try it out with a group of students. Find out students' reaction to the form. Does the form provide you with the information you require? How would you use the information you have collected?

What of the criteria for making overall judgements about reading ability? As with all other skills, the kind of judgement you make should reflect the kind of reading that you have been doing. For example, if students need to be able to read newspapers, magazines and informal letters, then you should expose them to these types of texts and assess their performance only on these texts. It would be unwise, unfair and unreliable to expose them only to magazines and then expect them to make a judgement about how well they read letters.

One sort of band you can use can be used in different situations as it does not specify the kinds of texts. You can use the band together with your own syllabus plan to assess students.

For example:

> **5** Can understand all necessary text types with no difficulty
> **4** Has minor difficulty with different text types
> **3** Has considerable difficulty with different text types
> **2** Cannot understand different text types
> **1** Cannot understand any text type

Another approach is to specify text types and use a *Yes/No* criteria.

For example:

1 Can understand factual articles in magazines

YES ☐

NO ☐

2 Can understand informal letters

YES ☐

NO ☐

> Choose five or six students from your class.
> During a reading activity in normal class hours, use the above rating scale for reading to assess your students' reading ability. If possible, use both the *holistic* scale and the *Yes/No* scales. Which do you prefer?

Grammar and vocabulary

As well as assessing students' performance and progress in terms of the four skills, it can also be useful to measure their knowledge and ability to use specific structures and vocabulary. This is an area which can probably be best assessed through periodical short progress tests but informal assessment can also be used.

Having presented a structure it is important to assess learners' understanding of it and ability to use it. This should be done at the practice stage of the lesson. During controlled practice activities you can go around the class and identify problems that students are having and observe which students are having particular difficulties. Having done this you may need to work out extra practice activities for all or some of the students in the class. To avoid dividing the class and establishing a special remedial group you can do further activities in groups, where the stronger students can help the weaker ones.

In addition to assessing students' knowledge and use of specific structures directly after presentation (in the language practice stages of a lesson), you may find it useful to assess students' grasp of structure and lexis in general while they are doing free writing and speaking activities. Rather than assess communication as a whole, which we have looked at in previous sections, you can focus solely on language. For example, in a speaking activity you could go around the class and write down the most important mistakes that the students are making. You can then go through the mistakes with the whole class, or alternatively plan remedial activities to deal with the problems.

As well as focusing on students' use of language you can also check their knowledge of it in an informal way. This is particularly useful before they have formal tests so that you can give them extra practice if necessary and they get an idea of what language they need to study more. One way of doing this is through class quizzes. You can divide the class up into groups and organise a competitive quiz between the groups, making sure first that each group has a balance between more and less able students. You can work out a series of questions to ask about both grammar and lexis and you can run the quiz in an enjoyable way, giving students bonus points, prizes etc. The sort of questions you can ask the groups are as follows:
'What is wrong with this sentence? My fathers are called John and Mary'. 'Make a sentence from these words.' 'What does bicycle mean in Spanish, Italian etc?'

In this informal way you can get an idea of your learners' knowledge and ability to use specific structures and lexis. Any problems that you diagnose through this sort of assessment can then be dealt with by remedial presentation or further practice. What you cannot get from the kind of informal assessment of language suggested here is an idea of individual students' knowledge and ability to use language. This is best done through short language tests spread out over the course.

1.4 Informal assessment of non-linguistic factors

We also need to think about our students' overall educational development. It is important for learners to develop in terms of a language and in terms of attitudes towards learning, towards language, different cultures and other people. We also need to consider students' ability to take responsibility for and organise their own learning. We need to consider how much importance we are going to give to non-linguistic factors. If we discount non-linguistic factors and only assess language, we can find ourselves passing those students who have done no work and have even been disruptive in class but who started with a higher level than most of the class. The converse could also be true.

Giving non-linguistic factors greater importance will encourage personal effort and achievement important in a mixed ability situation. However, we could be open to accusations that we are failing to reflect our students' linguistic performance and that we must assess students in relation to pre-established syllabus goals. The balance is a difficult one and how we solve it will depend on the particular teaching situation that we are in.

Assessing non-linguistic areas can also be a very difficult area to deal with in terms of reliability and fairness. If we say that a student has a poor attitude without having concrete evidence for it, we can lay ourselves open to accusations of partiality and unfairness. We need to be clear about the criteria we are using and provide proof to back up our decisions about non-linguistic factors.

We need to carry out systematic observation and to keep records of it, (eg attendance, participation in class etc). Students' work, eg compositions vocabulary books etc can be good indicators of attitudes and responsibility.

Informal assessment – Non-linguistic factors

Either on your own or with a colleague, decide which of the items below you think are important in terms of assessment. If you think that an item should be assessed, how could you assess it? If not, why not?

a Attitude
- is interested in class activities
- is willing to offer opinions
- is co-operative with teacher/peers
- is willing to respond to the opinions of others

b Co-operativeness
- is able to work in pairs
- is able to work in groups
- is able to work as a member of the whole class
- is able to share ideas and knowledge

c   Independence
- is able to plan and organise own work
- is able to self-correct where necessary
- is able to use sources of information

d Creativity and presentation
- shows original thought, initiative, inventiveness
- presents work neatly and in an ordered manner

We will introduce the factors first and then after initial discussion we will suggest a way of mapping the factors discussed onto a reporting system.

Attitude

We can look at attitudes towards learning, attitudes towards the language itself, attitudes towards other cultures and attitudes towards other people. The most important one is the first one, as without a positive attitude to learning, learning itself is not very likely to take place.

One way of assessing our students' attitude is by writing profiles.

Look at the two student profiles. Which one is the best student?

Student A

This student appears in the classroom to be a passive learner. He offers no opinions nor adds anything to any language discussion. Student A appears to be uninterested in everything that is going on around him. He seems bored. He does not co-operate with other members of the class. If involved in two-way communication, he interrupts his companions constantly and often dismisses their opinions, insisting that his opinions are right.

Student B

This student appears always to be actively involved in class activities. She always offers an opinion and enriches discussions with her views. Student B always appears to be interested in what is happening in the classroom. She appears to be stimulated by class activities. She co-operates with you the teacher and the rest of the class. She is a good listener and appears to accept her companions' viewpoints whilst at the same time giving her own at the appropriate moment in a conversation.

A judgement or rating could be made each month or term or academic year. Student A and B profiles identified the following areas as possible criteria for assessment:
◆ is passive/active
◆ offers opinions/does not offer opinions
◆ shows interest/does not show interest
◆ co-operates/does not co-operate
◆ accepts opinions/does not accept opinions

Other areas we could consider in terms of attitude are effort and interest. Here we can look at concrete indicators of effort and interest, eg whether a student hands in homework regularly when asked, whether a student is punctual, whether his/her attendance is regular and whether he/she reads in English outside the class.

Group work

In language classrooms the ability to work with other people in a group is crucial. It should also be one of our general educational objectives to develop the ability to co-operate with other people. Assessment of group work can be carried out in the same way as that of attitude and the following areas as assessment can be identified:

◆ has difficulty/does not have difficulty in groups
◆ co-operates/does not co-operate with group members
◆ is able to work in groups/only able to work alone
◆ accepts/rejects group organisation
◆ accepts/rejects the work of others

We also need to consider when to observe and collect our data – project work, role-plays and games all provide us with opportunities to observe and assess. Perhaps the most useful of these is project work when students need to work together to produce something. Co-operation will thus involve making decisions in groups, sharing out work, helping each other and positively criticising the work of others. As we will mention in the chapter on self-assessment, peer assessment can be a very good source of information about this. While you can observe students working together in the classroom you will not be aware of the dynamics of each group in the class.

Organisation of work

This is the ability of students to organise their own work, a very important learning skill which we need to help our students develop. Assessment can be carried out in the same way as the previous two factors and the following areas as assessment criteria can be identified:

◆ is able/unable to organise work systematically
◆ is able/unable to plan work
◆ is able/unable to produce presentable work
◆ is conscientious/not conscientious
◆ self-corrects/does not self-correct

Other things which we could take into consideration when looking at students' ability to organise their own work are the following: their notebook, their grammar notes and their vocabulary books. All of these are important indicators and one way of helping you assess this area could be to take them in and look at them. It is fairly easy to see their ability to organise their work from the way students write their notes and store lexis and grammar. It is worth pointing out however that if you do this you should give them some help to start with. Learner training activities at the beginning of the year should include looking at ways of organising learning such as establishing vocabulary books.

Independence

This is the ability of students to work on their own as well as part of a group (see under Group Work). Students should be encouraged and trained to work alone using resources available to them such as dictionaries, text books and other reference works. The following areas as assessment criteria can be identified:

◆ is able/unable to use dictionaries
◆ is able/unable to use the course text book as a resource
◆ is able/unable to refer back to previous work as an aid
◆ is able/unable to produce pieces of work without help

All the factors mentioned need to be mapped onto a rating scale if they are to be assessed with any degree of reliability. On the following page is a suggested model, taking as its criteria a YES/NO response to the areas identified in each non-linguistic factor above. The different criteria would be best separated out into four different scales with a decision made for each item.

Attitude	Is an active member of the class.	Yes/No
	Is able and willing to offer own opinions on subjects.	Yes/No
	Shows interest in class activities.	Yes/No
	Is generally co-operative with other people in class.	Yes/No
	Is capable of modifying opinions in the light of those of others	Yes/No

> Use the criteria suggested about group work, organisation of work and independence to write your own scales like those above for attitude.

1.5 Results from informal assessment

Once you have implemented your informal assessment programme you will have results in the form of information about your students. This information may be a set of numbers such as ratings for speaking, reading, listening and writing or a set of criteria which the student can or cannot meet such as working in groups, ability to produce work independently etc. In order to use these results, they will need to be recorded against each student's name, perhaps in a register or other notebook used for this purpose and should be accessible to your students, your institution and yourself.

As informal assessment forms just one part of the overall assessment programme, results could be periodically compared to those obtained from formal and self-assessment. If results from all three forms of assessment correlate highly, ie in general each part seems to give similar results, you might assume that a fairly reliable picture of a student's ability is being built up and that any decisions you make about that student will be based on solid foundations. If a particular student's results do not correlate, eg his/her results on informal assessment are greatly different to results on formal assessment, you will probably want to find out the reasons. It may be that this student is nervous when taking formal tests. If this pattern is repeated across all students' results, it may be that you need to take a look at the validity and reliability of your formal tests. Of course, if results from tests seem more consistent than those from your informal testing, you will need to think again about how you are assessing informally.

You may find that results from informal assessment of non-linguistic factors such as attitude or group work give you important information about a student or students. There may be an attitude problem against which measures need to be taken in your classroom teaching methods. In any case, information about students should be looked at in each individual case and should at all times feed back into the teaching and learning process.

As teachers involved in language learning, we are primarily concerned with linguistic aspects of our students' performance and competence. However, we should not lose sight of the fact that other non-linguistic factors can and do affect the strictly linguistic in a positive or negative manner. Our job as teachers must be to assess and through our assessment maximise the learning potential of our students in all aspects of their learning experience. Underestimating the extra-linguistic factors would be to ignore an important aspect of that experience. Assessing these non-linguistic factors and discussing these with your students should heighten their awareness of the importance of such factors and should thus aid the maximisation of that potential. It should not be forgotten that we are not solely concerned with language per se but in education in the broadest sense of the word.

Action points: informal assessment

1 As a result of reading this chapter are you going to make any changes in the ways you informally assess your students? If so, what are they?

2 How are you going to weight different areas?
(*For example*, listening 25%, reading 20% etc.)

3 How are you going to informally assess your students' receptive performance ie listening and reading?
   ◆ by giving an impression mark
   ◆ by collecting in marks from tasks
   ◆ by using a rating scale

4 How are you going to informally assess your students' productive performance ie speaking and writing?
   ◆ by giving an impression mark
   ◆ by collecting and adding together a series of impression marks
   ◆ by collecting and adding together a series of marks based on rating scales
   ◆ by using rating scales to assess overall performance

5 Are you going to take into consideration non-linguistic factors? Why/why not?

6 If yes to the previous question, how are you going to assess non-linguistic factors?
   ◆ by observing students in class and giving an impression mark
   ◆ by observing students in class and rating them using scales
   ◆ by collecting in vocabulary/notebooks and marking them
   ◆ by using peer assessment of group work

2 Formal assessment

2.1 Why test?

In this chapter we shall look at the reasons for testing our students and we shall examine some of the possible test types which we could use. The list of types of test is not intended to be exhaustive, but intends to give you a breakdown of the main types of test commonly used, their advantages and disadvantages and the contexts in which they are best put to use. The type of test we use will depend on the situation, the need and the purpose of testing.

Objections

Some common arguments against classroom testing (as opposed to informal assessment) are the following:

a *'Testing takes up valuable time which I could better use for teaching.'*
b *'I know how my students are doing anyway. Why do I need to test them as well?'*
c *'Some of the students in my class, who have worked hard all year, fail tests. Others who have done less work pass them, just because they have been to an English speaking country or because they have private classes.'*
d *'Tests do not motivate my students at all. The good ones feel complacent and the bad ones just give up.'*

Rationale

Here are some answers to the objections raised in a to d above:

a Testing takes up time, but it should be seen as part of the teaching/learning process rather than something divorced from it.
b This information is not always accurate, especially in the case of large classes. When students are working together in the classroom situation, individual weaknesses can be obscured. Tests therefore enable us to measure progress in a more individualised way.
c Tests are only part of the assessment process and should be seen as a complement to, eg self and informal assessment.
d Motivation will depend on how we use the results of the test. If tests are seen as competitive, they may demotivate students If they are seen as opportunities for students to find out how they are progressing, tests can motivate students to think about their problems and do something about them. Thus it is important for tests to be linked to self-assessment so they can add to other areas of formative assessment, assessment which helps our learners to develop.

Reasons for testing

Let us look in detail at why we should test our students. Firstly, whenever a test is administered, there is a decision to be made:

◆ We may want to find out about a candidate's suitability to follow a course of study, although this is not the case in state education.
◆ We may need to find out how a student is progressing during a course of study and possibly identify problem areas before a course ends.
◆ We may want to compare a student's performance with that of other students.
◆ We may want to find out how much a student has learned during the course or academic year ie compare what students can do at the end of the course compared with the beginning of the course.

In all these cases, decisions are made about the student. If no decision is to be made as a result of the test, there seems little point in administering the test. If you have a clear idea of the kind of decision which needs to be made about your learners, then you will be closer to identifying the most appropriate kind of test for you.

A common misconception, held by students and teachers alike, is that a test is something which is done *to* or *at* people rather than something which is done *by* them and *for* them. We should view the decisions which are made about students as decisions which are taken for them. Formal testing should be seen as a complement to other forms of assessment, eg self-assessment and informal assessment. The basic differences are that if we have a well designed, reliable and valid test, then the test will measure students' ability in a more objective way than more subjective forms of assessment such as informal observation and self-assessment. This is not to say that all formal testing is objective. Nor should we take the view that subjective is necessarily bad and that objective is necessarily good. For example all oral tests are subjectively marked and all multiple choice type tests are objectively marked.

The influence of tests on teaching and learning is called the *washback effect*. If your students have to do a test or maybe a public examination at the end of the course this will affect the syllabus. If we have a good test, this should affect teaching in a positive manner. If we have a bad test, this might affect teaching in a negative manner. What is a *'good'* test and what is a *'bad'* test? A test can have a positive influence if it contains authentic, real-life examples of the type of tasks which your learners will need to perform in the future. Tests can have a negative influence if they contain artificial tasks not linked to real future needs. Teaching methods will probably reflect these tasks and the learning process could end up revolving around what we might term 'exam practice'. Your own tests will also have an effect on your students' learning. If you test mainly grammar, your students will assume that this is the most important thing to learn and may make less effort during other more communicative activities.

Washback effect

Match these examples of assessment with their washback effects:

1 A progress test which concentrates on one out of four chapters covered in the textbook.

Good washback. Students will feel they have been tested fairly.

2 An end of year test which concentrates on grammar and vocabulary, even though you have done lots of speaking and listening.

Good washback. The information will help you plan your course to suit the needs of your students.

3 A diagnostic test which has shown that your class is very weak on speaking skills.

Bad washback. Students will feel that luck was more important than hard work.

4 An end of year test of reading, listening and speaking, covering a wide range of material.

Bad washback. Students will feel that classwork has been a waste of time.

Check your answers on page 61

When we are testing we also need to ask ourselves who the test is for and who will look at the results. We therefore need to think about who we are accountable to. Firstly we must think about our learners who need to receive feedback about progress and performance. They will compare the test and the test methods to the teaching methods you have used. Therefore it is important for us to tell them how we are going to test them at the beginning of a course and perhaps tell them why we are going to test them like this.

In most schools parents will use test results as a way of determining student's progress, interest and application to the course of study. Parents will also consider results, especially those from public examinations, as evidence of the effectiveness of the teacher, teaching methods and school. Test results should therefore be easily accessible and comprehensible to parents of students. We should be able to explain to parents how we got the results and our rationale for testing in this way.

Types of test

Before, during and at the end of courses, different types of test are administered. The key question is the purpose of the test. Different tests are administered for different purposes and are used at different stages of the course as a means of gathering information about students. The main types of test are discussed below and the pros and cons of each type are described. However, you, as language teachers, should decide on what the best option is in each instance for your particular group(s) of learners and your particular teaching situation.

Progress tests

This type of test is administered during courses. Progress tests may be administered after certain blocks of study, eg after *x* number of units, at the end of each week, each term etc. The test aims to find out information about how well classes as a whole and individual students have grasped the learning objectives, how well the course content is functioning within the specified aims and objectives and future course design. Teachers can easily identify how well students are progressing in a very short period of time, eg a progress test of half an hour can give a great deal of information about the class if the test is well designed. Progress tests can provide a great deal of information if the test samples widely from the course content. Progress tests can perform a very important formative function in that they do not only give information to the teacher but can provide important feedback to the student. When linked with self-assessment, feedback can help learners to identify their own problems and to set their own goals for the future.

Summative tests

These tests are administered at the end of courses and their objective is to see if students have achieved the objectives set out in the syllabus. While these tests can be used effectively as a way of deciding whether students move on to a higher level, this can be done better at secondary school level by progress tests throughout the year in combination with informal assessment by the teacher. A lot of information gained from a summative test is often wasted because it does not feed back into the learning process as does formative assessment. Also, end of year tests can put a lot of stress on both teachers and students.

Entry/placement tests

This type of test will indicate at which level a learner will learn most effectively in a situation where there are different levels or streams. The aim is to produce groups which are homogeneous in level that will use institutional and teacher time most effectively. The larger the groups of learners to be designed, the more homogeneous the groups will need to be and therefore the more reliable the entry or placement test will need to be. This type of test is less useful where students are grouped alphabetically or according to age rather than ability. Entry or placement tests are not very common in state run institutions.

Diagnostic test

As the name suggests, this type of test is used to find out problem areas. Where other types of tests are based on success, diagnostic tests are based on failure. We want to know in which areas a student or group of students are having problems, which parts of a course or learning objectives those students cannot cope with. One way of looking at this type of test is to consider it as a technique based on eliciting errors rather than correct answers or language.

Diagnostic information is vital for teachers in order to design further course activities and work out remedial activities. The information can also be useful for learners, as they can analyze their own problems. Diagnostic testing is present in many progress tests for the simple reason that the progress tests identify problem areas. However, a reliable diagnostic test is difficult to design.

Proficiency tests

This type of test aims to describe what students are capable of doing in a foreign language and are usually set by external bodies such as examination boards. Proficiency tests enable students to have some proof of their ability in a language. They also provide potential employers with some guarantee of proficiency in a language because examination boards are seen as bodies which set standards in an impartial way and boards' examinations are generally considered to be reliable and valid. Some proficiency tests, while claiming to be communicative, often have a large language component such as grammar or vocabulary. This can have a negative washback effect on teaching in terms of examination preparation.

Your testing

Which of these questions do you need to answer about your students?
- What levels they should go into?
- How are they getting on at the moment?
- What are their problems and weaknesses?
- How much have they learnt over the course?
- What can my students do in English?

What types of test do you have to do? Match these types with the questions:
summative / diagnostic / proficiency / placement / progress
Check your answers on page 61

2.2 Planning assessment programmes

Having taken the decision to assess students formally, it is vital to do it systematically. It is not enough to test students in a piecemeal way, as the need arises. We need to plan a clear assessment programme at the beginning of the academic year. First, we need to think about our syllabus objectives and work out a programme, thinking about what we are going to test and when. Then we need to decide how we are going to test and choose the most suitable test formats for our purpose. Having done this we can actually start to write tests and administer them. Finally, we need to think about the results and use them to come to conclusions about our learners' progress.

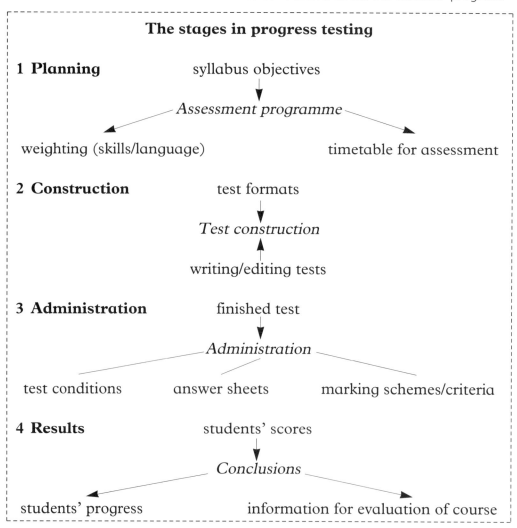

The stages in progress testing

1 Planning   syllabus objectives
↓
Assessment programme
↙   ↘
weighting (skills/language)   timetable for assessment

2 Construction   test formats
↓
Test construction
↑
writing/editing tests

3 Administration   finished test
↓
Administration
↙   ↓   ↘
test conditions   answer sheets   marking schemes/criteria

4 Results   students' scores
↓
Conclusions
↙   ↘
students' progress   information for evaluation of course

When are we going to test?

Traditionally, exams are at the end of term or at the end of year. Students are under great pressure and often do not do their best; teachers are snowed under with preparation of exams and then vast amounts of marking. The crucial decisions of pass and fail are often taken during, or in the aftermath of this period. The end of term exam thus has several major disadvantages:

◆ Students and teachers are under stress. For the teacher a large amount of work is concentrated into a short period of time. For the student, if he or she has a bad day, the work done throughout the year is questioned. Thus the end of term exam is often not a representative sample of students' performance over the course. Used as the only instrument it can result in unreliable assessment.

◆ The diagnostic information from the exams is usually discarded. What we learn about students' weaknesses and problems comes very late and is often forgotten in the end of term rush. At the start of the following term this information is hardly ever checked up on and used by the next teacher of the class.

◆ Students themselves are much too worried about their results to think about the difficulties they had, or reflect on the progress they made.

◆ In the eyes of the students, assessment is divorced from learning. Exam technique, luck on the day and the ability to write quickly are qualities prized more than hard work, interest and enthusiasm.

◆ The period after exams is a kind of academic no-man's-land between school and the holidays; the teacher has to occupy large groups of distracted and potentially disruptive adolescents whose motivation to study is low.

To overcome some of the problems related to end of term exams it is possible to balance your formal assessment with the informal assessment you have been doing throughout the term. This helps to take into account the fact that students could have had a bad day when they did the test. You can also make sure that you go through the exams thoroughly with your students, making sure that they receive adequate feedback about their problems. Students can reflect on the problems they had and you can set remedial work for them (perhaps to do over the holidays). It is also worth considering an alternative to the end of term exam: a series of short 'assessment tasks' to take place throughout the term. The time spent assessing formally is the same, but this time is a great deal more productive.

Here is an example of an assessment task programme:

Assessment tasks: Autumn term
Week 1: Writing task (20 min) To find out what students have remembered after the holidays or find out about new students and their weaknesses.
Week 3: Listening task (15 min) Something fairly easy to build confidence. A listening task well within students' reach, (eg short dialogue).
Week 4: Reading task A text related to one of the topic areas being looked at, (eg picture story/cartoon).
Week 6: Language assessment task To check on grammar and vocabulary studied so far.
Week 8: Writing task To check one of the writing areas looked at so far, (eg informal letters).
Week 9: Listening task More challenging task and text than the first one, (eg story/longer dialogue).
Week 11: Reading task More challenging task and text than the first one, (eg extract from children's non-fiction).
Week 12: Language assessment task To check on the grammar and vocabulary studied since the previous language task.

Total time spent 150 minutes

This system has considerable advantages over the traditional end of term exam. Firstly, there is less stress for both students and teachers. If a student has a bad day, he/she has a chance to do better another day. Thus, the 'assessment task' system should provide a much more accurate picture of students' ability. Secondly, the work involved in preparing tests and correcting them is spread over the term, instead of being concentrated into one hectic period. Reliability in marking should be correspondingly enhanced. Thirdly, the assessment tasks provide vital diagnostic data for the teacher, which can then feed back into the course. In addition, students get very useful information about how they are doing throughout the course. Assessment tasks avoid the divorce between testing and teaching that end of term exams often produce. As well as taking place during the learning period, tasks can be related to the topic areas being studied. At the same time as measuring progress, tasks can be interesting and fun. If the thematic area being covered is 'Animals', a reading task on polar bears could extend students' knowledge. Finally, with a system of assessment tasks, there is no 'post-exam' period. It is however an idea to give a task right near the end which students have to do, to avoid students missing classes to study for other exams, or discuss with teachers of other subjects the idea of giving up end of term exams completely.

Planning an assessment programme

Look at the example of the assessment task programme on page 31. Choose one of your classes and plan your own programme of assessment tasks for a term. Write out the number of weeks in the term and then space formal assessment tasks as you see fit.

What are we going to test?

An important thing is to decide on weighting between different elements in the course. This will depend on the kind of class you have and the syllabuses you are following. If you pay a lot of attention to writing and grammar, your formal assessment should reflect this and you should test in the same way. If, on the other hand, you concentrate largely on speaking and listening, you should test mainly these.

While this may seem obvious, it is surprising how often 'communicative' classes have tests which are grammar-based. This has a very negative washback effect on students. They quite naturally come to feel that while speaking and listening are good fun, what really matters is grammar.

When planning formal assessment at classroom level it is useful to make a clear breakdown of what you are going to test and how much weight each area carries. This breakdown should clearly reflect the overall syllabus balance of your course.

For example:

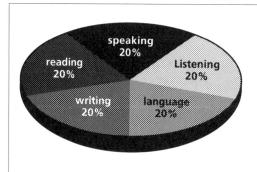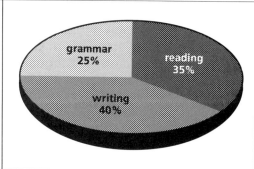

Assessment weighting

Look at the example of weighting on page 32. Draw a pie graph illustrating how you weight your formal assessment for one of your classes. Does it reflect your syllabus objectives? If it does not, change the weighting for the next time that you organise your programme.

Having decided on weighting, we need to establish priorities. We cannot test everything that students have done throughout the course. We must therefore look at our syllabuses and choose a sample of areas to assess formally.

Syllabus priorities

Look at the example of syllabus priorities below, for 13/14 year old post-elementary students. Then list your own priorities for your classes. Think about the following areas:
- speaking
- listening
- reading
- writing
- grammar
- vocabulary

Syllabus objectives

Speaking	general fluency/ability to talk about own life (likes/dislikes/homes/food/past)
Listening	extensive listening – (listening for gist and for specific information) stories/dialogues/radio programmes
Reading	extensive reading – skimming/scanning/dictionary use magazines/comics/children's fiction/non-fiction
Writing	writing about own lives – letters/stories/postcards
Grammar	revision and introduction of: present simple /continuous, past simple, present perfect, future: going to, countables
Lexis	lexical areas: classroom/animals/homes/travel

2.3 Choosing test formats

Having worked out a general assessment programme, the next step is to decide how we are going to test. At this stage it is important to refer once more to some of the fundamental concepts in assessment.

◆ Firstly, we want our assessment tasks to be *reliable*. This means that they should be *consistent* measures of students' performance. If the same test were given under the same conditions on a different day, the results should be the same.

◆ Secondly, we must ensure that our assessment tasks have *validity*, they test what we want them to, rather than testing something else. For example, a reading test where answers are marked for grammatical accuracy is not only a test of reading. It is a test of writing and grammar as well.

◆ Thirdly, our assessment tasks need to be *practical*. They must not take too long to do or mark, be too difficult to organise or involve equipment and resources that we do not possess.

◆ Lastly, it should be clear to our students that our tests reflect what we are doing in class, thus hopefully causing a *positive washback* effect on learning. If tasks assess communicative ability, our students will be encouraged to take part in communicative activities. If they test grammar, our students will see skills work as peripheral to the main job of learning grammar.

In an ideal world, our assessment tasks would be extremely practical and reliable, with high validity and a beneficial *washback effect*. In practice however, this is not so easy to achieve. If we want high reliability, *discrete item* test formats are the most suitable. These are formats with many items requiring short answers, (eg – multiple choice questions). Because there are more items, we have more information available to us and *reliability* is increased. These test formats are also very practical, usually being quick and easy to mark. Unfortunately, such formats can have low *validity*, because doing a test such as a multiple choice is not a test of real communication.

Such discrete item tasks can also have a *negative washback effect*, with the test-wise student often doing best. On the other hand, if we want high validity, *integrative* and *open-ended* test formats can be better. Integrative formats involve communication and interaction (for example reading a letter and replying to it). Open-ended formats are those where responses are open, (eg written compositions such as stories).

Both of these formats can have *beneficial washback effects*, as students become aware of the importance of communication. However, it can be difficult to interpret results from such open-ended tests. Firstly, it can be hard to decide why students had problems (was it the reading or the writing?). Secondly, these tests can be impractical, taking a long time to mark and administer. Thirdly, they can be unreliable, as they are much more difficult to mark consistently than discrete item tests. Thus, we have a certain dilemma as to how we are going to test.

1 Discrete item formats

2 Integrative/open-ended formats

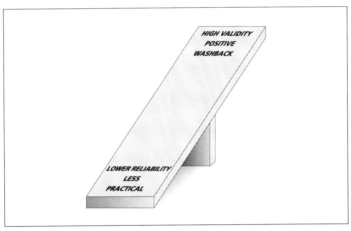

As both discrete item and integrative test formats have their advantages and disadvantages, perhaps the solution is to mix the kinds of test formats we use. We could employ some integrative tasks, especially for productive skills like writing and speaking. For the receptive skills and for testing language, we could use some discrete item tasks. Our discrete item formats make it easier for us to assess with greater reliability and with less time for marking. Our more open-ended formats enable us to give our students tests of real communication. However, we need to look in more detail at what kind of test format best fits our specific requirements.

Reviewing test formats

1 Read through the list of test formats. List those that you use.
2 Look through it again and make a list of other activities that you use in class and that might be interesting for you to use in your tests in the future. Ask these questions:
a Will it help me test reliably what I want to test?
b Have I got enough time and resources to use it?
c If I use it will it have a good effect on my students and reinforce my syllabus objectives?

Survey of test formats

Abbreviations:

IQ – intelligence quotient: a commonly used measurement of intelligence

ss – students   info – information   dk – don't know

Reading and listening

TEST FORMAT	PROS	CONS
Short answer questions eg 'How tall are elephants?' 'Three metres.'	*Easy to write and mark. Very good for checking gist or intensive understanding of texts.*	*Some writing. Important not to mark for accuracy and to decide what answers are correct. Need to ensure q's do not test ss' knowledge of the world.*
Table completion eg 'Complete the table with information.' (age / family etc).	*Easy to construct and mark. Good for checking specific info or data form a text.*	*Some writing. Need to decide on what answers accepted as correct.*
Diagrams/maps/pictures eg 'Label the places on the map'	*Quite realistic, motivating tasks. Good for checking specific info.*	*Can be difficult to draw pictures. Could involve non-linguistic skills (eg map reading).*
Listing eg 'List the kinds of food mentioned in the text'.	*Realistic. Easy to write and mark. Better for listening than reading.*	*Tests recognition of words. Does not test understanding or meaning.*
True, false, don't know eg 'Mark the sentences t/f or dk: Lions are cats.'	*Easy to write. Quite realistic. Tests gist or intensive understanding well.*	*High guessing element: 50% for t/f, 33% for t/f/dk.*
Multiple choice eg 'Choose the correct answer: John goes out.- a sometimes b rarely c never.'	*Very easy to mark thus good for very large classes. Good for checking gist or intensive understanding.*	*Very difficult to construct. Wrong options (distracters) can distract better students. Guessing element.*
Sequencing (texts/ pictures) eg 'Listen and put the paragraphs in order.'	*Easy to construct. Good for stories (listening) and for linking of discourse.*	*Very difficult to mark. If one answer is wrong, others are too. Impractical unless marking scheme is adapted.*
Text Completion eg 'Listen and complete the information about the film.'	*Quite realistic. Good for listening for specific info.*	*For reading it tests knowledge of language. (see close and gap-fill)*
Problem solving eg 'From the following info work out the people's names'	*Realistic and good fun. Tests global understanding.*	*Can test general IQ not ability to read or listen.*
Word attack eg 'Work out the meaning of these words from the text.'	*Tests ability to infer meaning from context (for reading).*	*NOT suitable for listening (when it can work as a vocabulary test).*
Identify topic (text/paragraph) eg 'Match the title with the text.'	*Good for gist reading. Easy to construct and mark.*	*Need to think of suitable answers when questions are open (eg giving titles to texts).*
Linking eg 'What does the underlined word refer to? It arrived late.'	*Good for testing intensive understanding / linking within text. (cohesion)*	*Need to underline words and give line numbers to make task easier to do and mark.*
Identify linking words in a text eg after/next etc	*Good for working out how a text holds together. (cohesion)*	*Can be more a test of word recognition than of understanding.*
Discrepancies eg 'Read the text then listen and list the differences.'	*Realistic, integrative test of both reading and listening.*	*Difficult to see if problems are due to listening or reading.*

Writing

TEST FORMAT	PROS	CONS
Essay questions eg 'Write about a day when everything went wrong.'	*Very easy to set. Better for higher levels.*	*Very unrealistic and often tests imagination or content knowledge. Difficult and time consuming to mark.*
Guided writing Using pictures, notes, diagrams (giving ss some input of info)	*More realistic than essays, because input can create reason for communication. Gives students help, thus good for lower levels. Easier to mark than free writing.*	*Input can be a test of reading – if ss do not understand input this will affect their writing.*
Punctuation (punctuating texts)	*Good for testing specific knowledge of punctuation.*	*Restricted and not easy to mark – punctuation can be subjective (related to style).*
Summary eg 'Read the text and summarise it in 20 lines.'	*A realistic, integrative task. Tests both reading and writing.*	*Difficult to mark. (What is important in a text can be subjective)*
Note taking eg 'Read the text and write notes.'	*A realistic and useful task for ss to practise.*	*Can be difficult to mark unless it is guided.*
Dictation eg 'Listen and write down the text.'	*Realistic. A good integrative test of listening and writing (spelling).*	*Very difficult to mark, unless a very clear scheme is established.*
Combined eg 'Read the letter and write a reply.'	*Realistic and very good for writing.*	*Difficult to mark-to distinguish between problems in reading or writing*

Speaking

TEST FORMAT	PROS	CONS
Free interviews (chat to ss in groups or as individuals)	*Realistic and can reduce stress for ss.*	*Very difficult to rate performance (personality factor – shy /outgoing). Need to maintain conversation at same time as rating.*
Picture description (using photo or drawing)	*Gives tester time to listen and ss something concrete.*	*Artificial task and there is no interaction.*
Information transfer (information gap through notes or pictures)	*Realistic – need for communication. Tests key interactive strategies.*	*Can be problems when one student is a lot weaker than the other. (doesn't work)*
Roleplay Ss assume roles (with or without cued info)	*Excellent for testing interaction and commonly used task in most materials.*	*Can test the ability to act.*
Oral presentations Ss prepare and give short talks.	*Realistic and gives the tester time to assess performance.*	*No interaction and can have a high stress factor – not suitable for younger ss.*

Language

TEST FORMAT	PROS	CONS
Cloze Blank out every nth word (5th/6th) in a reading text. Ss complete the blanks	*Easy to construct (a text and a bottle of liquid paper).*	*Can test IQ more than language (puzzle element). Can be irritating for ss.*
Gap-fill Selected words in a text are blanked out. Ss have to fill in the blanks.	*Good for testing different structures, provides clear contexts. Easy to write and mark.*	*Need to think about possible answers.*
Word sequencing, eg 'Order the words below to make sentences.'	*Excellent for testing structures with problems of word order (eg-questions).*	*Can be difficult to mark (some mistakes worse than others). Contains puzzle element.*
Editing Ss correct mistakes.	*Realistic. Good for testing L1 interference.*	*Can be too difficult if mistakes are not signalled.*
Cued sentences (from pictures or words)	*Easy to write and mark.*	*Can be mechanical – repeated use of same structure.*
Personalisation, eg 'Write five sentences about your family.' Writing short texts eg 'Write a dialogue with these words.'	*Easy to write. Good for some functions (eg likes /dislikes) Tests usage of structures beyond sentence level.*	*Can be mechanical. Can be difficult to mark (open-ended). Need for clear criteria.*
Identifying structures eg tenses/parts of speech	*Tests knowledge of grammatical system and of metalanguage*	*Does not test usage of structures.*
Translation eg 'Translate these sentences into English.'	*Tests problems of form and usage caused by L1 interference.*	*Many ss and teachers feel that the target language only should be used.*
Table completion eg 'Complete the table with these adjectives.'	*Good for testing knowledge of irregulars and word-building*	*Mechanical – does not test usage.*
Sentence transformation eg 'Finish the sentences so that they mean the same.'	*Good for testing some structures (eg-passives /conditionals)*	*Very artificial and can test IQ as well as language.*
Lexis classification eg 'Match the words with the topics.'	*Good for testing lexical sets.*	*Does not test usage of vocabulary.*
Matching sentence halves (one half of a sentence with the other)	*Good for testing some structures (eg conditionals / gerunds and infinitives).*	*Need numbers and letters to make it easier to mark.Eg 2 – c*
Matching words / definitions	*Good for specific words and link with dictionary skills.*	*Does not involve usage of vocabulary.*

Identifying test formats

Look at the examples of the assessment tasks on the next few pages. Identify the formats used in the tasks. Check your answers on page 62.

Example Task 1 Combined (reading/writing)

Examples of test formats

Assessment task 1 Writing (elementary)

Read this letter from a penfriend and reply to it. Include this information about yourself: Name Age Family Where you live Hobbies Favourite sports Music

> 15 Newmarket Rd,
> Scunthorpe,
> Great Britain.
>
> 10th June.
>
> Dear......,
> Hi! My name's Rodney and I'm your new penfriend. I am thirteen and I've got four sisters!!! (Sammy, Karen, Angie and Kim) My mum's called Doris and she works in a bank. My dad, Rodney, is a mechanic. We live in a town called Scunthorpe. It is really boring and I don't like it very much. Before we lived in Manchester.
>
> I've got lots of hobbies. I collect pens (now I've got 450 of them!). Also I make model aeroplanes. I don't like sport very much, but I like table tennis. I am really good at it!! My favourite music is heavy metal and my favourite group is The Electric Chameleons.
>
> What about you? Write to me and tell me about your hobbies and sports.
>
> Bye!
>
> Rodney

Marking criteria

Give an impression mark out of ten. Use this rating scale to help you:

9/10 Communicates all the relevant information and is interesting to read. Hardly any mistakes of grammar, lexis, spelling or punctuation.

7/8 Communicates the information needed. Few mistakes of grammar, lexis, spelling or punctuation.

5/6 Communicates most of the information needed. Quite a few mistakes, but it is possible to understand.

3/4 A lot of the information is not communicated and mistakes make it difficult to understand.

1/2 Has communicated very little.

Assessment task 2 Writing (beginner)

Use the notes to write a description of the animal.

Example:
'Her name is Booboo and she is a small animal. She is...'

Name

Age

10

Family

Lives in

Favourite food

Favourite music

Likes

Dislikes

Marking criteria
Give a mark out of five for the information included and a mark out of five for accuracy (mistakes in terms of grammar and lexis)

Assessment task 3 Reading (elementary)

You can use dictionaries for this task.

1 Read the information about chameleons. Match the titles with the paragraphs (1,2 and 3). (3pts)

a Eyes, tongues and tails. b Colour changes. c Insect hunters.

2 Read it again and complete this table (4pts)

Name of animal	What they eat
Where they live	Their colour

3 Why can chameleons catch insects? List three reasons (3pts)

1 *Chameleons are lizards that live in Africa and the island of Madagascar. They can't move very fast and they are not very intelligent, but they hunt insects like flies and mosquitoes which are very fast. How do they do it?*

2 *First, chameleons can move their eyes in different directions. They can look in front of them and behind them at the same time! They have special tails, so that they can hold onto things and they have very long tongues which can catch the insects.*

3 *But best of all, the poor insects cannot see them, because chameleons can completely change colour. If they are sitting in a tree, they can turn brown and green. If they are sitting on a grey stone, they can turn grey. So, when a chameleon feels hungry it just has to sit and wait for its lunch to fly past!*

Marking scheme (task 3)

Section 1: one point for every correct answer:
a 2   b 3   c 1

Section 2: one point for every correct answer
Name of animal: chameleon
Where they live: Africa/Madagascar
What they eat: insects (flies/mosquitoes)
Their colour: green/grey/brown different colours

Section 3: three points
Students do not have to write complete sentences. Notes are fine. Do not penalise students for bad spelling, grammar etc.
Chameleons can move eyes/see in front and behind them at the same time. They have long tongues. They can change colour/insects can't see them.

Assessment task 4 Listening (post-elementary)
Listen to the story of the tortoise and the hare.
a Decide if the sentences are true (T), false (F), or there is no information about them (NI).

Example: The tortoise and the hare lived in the old house. NI
  1 The tortoise wanted to have a race.
  2 The distance was one kilometre.
  3 A lot of animals came to watch the race.
  4 The race happened in September.

b Listen again and answer these questions.

Example: What time were they ready to start the race?   3.55
  5 When did the race start?
  6 When did the hare stop?
  7 What time did he go to sleep?
  8 What time did the tortoise go past him?
  9 When did the hare wake up?
10 What time did the tortoise cross the winning line?

| 4.00 | 4.10 | 4.15 | 4.50 | 4.59 | 5.00 |

Tapescript

Once upon a time there was a hare. He could run very fast and he wanted to race with all the other animals in the forest. One day he decided to have a race with the tortoise. He thought it would be very funny, because the tortoise was very, very slow. The hare was sure that he would win. The tortoise didn't want to race but finally the hare persuaded her. The hare invited all the animals of the forest to come and see the race. The race was between the old house and the river, a distance of about one kilometre.

All the animals of the forest came and at five to four they were ready. The race started at exactly four o'clock. The hare ran down the hill very fast. After ten minutes he was near the river, near the end of the race. But it was a very hot day and he decided to sit down and wait for the tortoise to come past. He sat down under a tree and because it was hot he felt sleepy. He went to sleep at a quarter past four.

Meanwhile, the tortoise was going slowly on. Finally, after fifty minutes she arrived at the tree where the hare was sleeping. She looked at him and carried on, towards the river.

A few minutes later, at one minute to five, the hare woke up. He ran very fast and in one minute he was at the winning line. But, just as he arrived, at exactly five o'clock, the tortoise crossed the line. She had won the race!!!!

Marking scheme
One point for each answer: Total out of ten.
    1F   2 T   3 T   4 NI   5 4.00pm   6 4.10   7 4.15 8 4.50   9 4.59   10 5.00

Assessment task 5 Speaking (elementary)

Part 1

Student A:

Find out this information about your partner:
name/age/family/favourite music/what s/he does at the weekends

Student B:

Find out this information about your partner:
name/age/hobbies/favourite school subject /what s/he does in the holidays

Part 2

Student A:

Describe this half of the picture to your partner. Then listen to his/her description and draw the rest of the picture. You can ask him/her questions

Student B:

Listen to your partner's description of the other half of the picture and draw it. You can ask him/her questions. Then describe the other half to him/her.

Part 3

Student A:

• Imagine that you are a journalist interviewing a famous film star. Ask him/her about these things: family/home/dislike/hobbies/plans for the future
• Imagine that you are a famous tennis player. Think about these things: family / home / hobbies / ambitions /plans
Then answer the journalist's questions

Student B:

• Imagine that you are a famous film star. Think about these things: family /home /likes / dislikes/hobbies/plans
Then answer the journalist's questions
• Imagine that you are a journalist interviewing a famous tennis player. Ask him/her about these things: family/home/hobbies/ambitions/plans for the future

Administration

Students to be interviewed in pairs. If possible, interview students away from the rest of the class (though you could do it at the front while the others get on with something else). Let them choose who they want to do the interview with.

Before the interviews, tell the students the components of the interview:
• personal information (warmer)
• picture description (information gap)
• roleplay

If the interview is taking too long and you feel that you have already seen enough you can miss out one of the above components (eg picture description).

Then explain to them the criteria that you will be using to assess them. During the interview, try to say as little as possible. However, help students if there is a breakdown in communication.
Use this scale to assess students:

Oral assessment rating scale

/5 FLUENCY	/5 ACCURACY
5 Tasks done very well Little hesitation	Correct use of structures studied so far. Clear pronunciation
4 Tasks done quite well Some hesitation	Use of different structures covered so far. Not many mistakes Pronunciation quite clear
3 Tasks done adequately Quite a few pauses	Use of some of the structures covered. Some mistakes, but reasonable understanding possible Pronunciation satisfactory
2 Tasks not done adequately A lot of hesitation	Structure and lexis limited. A lot of mistakes. Poor pronunciation
1 Response completely inadequate	Almost incomprehensible

Assessment task 6 Speaking (Intermediate)
Students perform the task on page 45 in pairs. One student is given Task Sheet A and the other student is given Task Sheet B.

Task Sheet A

You are a member of the two person student committee at your school responsible for student facilities. Your partner is the other member of the committee. The school has asked the committee to present a proposal on how best to spend money available for next year on different facilities and whether some facilities should be discontinued. In your opinion, the school should spend money on:
- more books for the library (there are too few at present)
- more equipment for the science block (present material is very old)
- more sports equipment (there is hardly any at present)
- more cultural trips (eg theatre, museums, local parks)
- more extra-curricular activities with other schools in the area

In your opinion, the following should be discontinued:
- student café (too expensive and not used very much)
- school magazine (very little interest and participation)
- daily newspaper (nobody reads it)
- parent/teacher association (hardly any interest)
- school swimming lessons (everyone learns outside school anyway)

Discuss all the above points with your partner and come to an agreement on what the proposal will be. You start by asking your partner what he/she thinks about the library.

Task Sheet B

You are a member of the two person student committee at your school responsible for student facilities. Your partner is the other member of the committee. The school has asked the committee to present a proposal on how best to spend money available for next year on different facilities and whether some facilities should be discontinued. In your opinion, the school should spend money on:
- student café (people would use it if it were cheaper)
- school magazine (it needs somebody to get people interested)
- daily newspaper (students should know about current affairs)
- parent/teacher association (very useful for solving problems)
- school swimming lessons (some students do not learn outside)

In your opinion, the following should be discontinued:
- library (very little interest and the books are all old)
- equipment for the science block (present material is sufficient)
- sports equipment (most students practice sports outside school)
- cultural trips (students are here to learn not to travel)
- extra-curricular activities with other schools in the area

Discuss all the above points with your partner and come to an agreement on what the proposal will be. Your partner will start by asking your opinion about one of the above points.

Oral rating scales

Below are examples of rating scales for use with the example of an oral test on page 45. After using the rating scales, consider the following questions and discuss with a colleague if possible:

1 Are the scales easy to use?
2 Did the scales become easier to use after rating 3 or 4 performances?
3 Could the scales be integrated to form one holistic scale?

Communication
5 Fluent communication
4 Good communication
3 Satisfactory communication
2 Communication hesitant
1 Communication minimal

Pronunciation and structure
5 Clear pronunciation and wholly appropriate use of structure
4 Few inaccuracies of structure and pronunciation
3 Inaccuracies of structure and pronunciation do not seriously impede understanding
2 Inaccuracies of structure and pronunciation impede understanding
1 Inaccuracies of structure and pronunciation make understanding almost impossible

Vocabulary
5 Wholly appropriate for task
4 Few limitations
3 Sometimes limited
2 Limitations affected task considerably
1 Inadequate for task

Assessment task 7
Language (elementary)
Total /30

a   Complete the description with these prepositions: (10pts)

at   (3)
in   (5)
on
from
by

Example:
Kristen Eriksen comes..from.. a small town near Oslo, 1.... Norway.
She gets up early, 2.... about 6.30, because her school starts 3.... 8.00
am. She usually goes to school 4.... bus and sometimes her dad takes
her. After school she often goes to the sports centre. She loves
swimming and playing tennis. Then, 5.... the evenings she does
homework and watches television.

6.... the weekends she doesn't have to get up early. 7....
Sunday mornings she goes to the country with her family. 8....
the winter they ski and 9.... the summer they go for long walks.
Sometimes, 10.... July and August, they go to the coast. But Kristen
doesn't swim, because the water is very cold!

b   Write questions about Kristen for these answers: (10pts)
Example:
Near Oslo. Where does Kristen live?
1 At 6.30 in the morning. ....?
2 Usually by bus. ....?
3 To the sports centre. ....?
4 No, she doesn't get up early. ....?
5 She goes with her family. ....?

c   Correct these mistakes. (5pts)
Example:
She gets at school by bus.
She gets to school by bus.
1 Kristen's brother studys at university.
2 What time do get you up?
3 How long does you take to go to school?
4 How is the weather in August?
5 It is snow a lot in the winter.

d Find the words for these pictures (5pts)

Example:
sunny

1 ....

2 ....

3 ....

4 ....

5 ....

Marking scheme

a One point for each answer
1 in   2 at   3 at   4 by   5 in   6 at   7 on   8 in   9 in   10 in

b Two points for each correct sentence. If there is only one small mistake (not related to word order and use of auxiliaries) give one out of two. Possible alternatives in brackets. (10pts)
1 What time does she (usually) get up in the morning? (during the week)
2 How does she (usually) go (get) to school?
3 Where does she go after school?
4 Does she get up early at the weekend? (on Saturday and Sunday)
5 Who does she go (with) to the country with?

c One point for each correction
1 studies
2 do you get
3 does it take you
4 what.... like
5 snows

d One point for each word
1 windy
2 cold
3 snowy
4 hot
5 rainy

2.4 Writing, administering and marking tests

As a teacher, you may often find that you are expected to write, administer and mark tests. All of these tasks can be time-consuming and we need to produce practical tests which can assess our students as reliably as possible in the time that we have available to us.

Writing tests

When we start writing tests we need to avoid confusion and ambiguity which may make our test unreliable or invalid. Having done an initial draft of the test we then need to check what we have done. Firstly, we should do the test ourselves to see if we can spot any changes that need to be made. Secondly, we can ask a colleague to do the test. What may be obvious to you may not be so obvious to another person - a colleague should help advise you on other changes. One way of testing writing which can make this process easier is by writing your tests with other colleagues from the beginning. First you should agree on what you want to test. Then you can either divide up the work (one person to do a listening test, another a reading test) or you can sit down and work on each test together. A collective approach to writing tests makes this difficult task easier and at the same time it provides you with an opportunity to compare ideas and attitudes. It is also an excellent time to discuss the criteria that you are going to use to assess performance in the tests. This of course assumes that time is available for these activities - you may have to compromise.

The first area to think about is that of writing instructions. It is very easy to concentrate only on the content of the test itself and to forget that students will need to know what to do during the test. Students only know what they have to do during the test by reading or hearing the instructions - this is often called the rubric. You may have a test which appears to be practical and valid, but without a clear and concise rubric the test will soon lose its validity if students are unclear as to what is expected of them.

Clarity is essential in rubrics. The rubric should tell the students exactly what they have to do, how they have to do it and what the marker is looking for. If the language is unclear, students may not know what is expected of them and could fail to perform to their full capability in the test.

> Consider which of the following rubrics is clearer, a or b:
> a Listen to the tape and put the right answer to the questions.
> b Listen to the tape and answer questions 1–10 below by putting a cross (X) in the correct box next to each question.

In the above cases, rubric b is clearer, as it tells students what they have to write and where they have to write it whereas rubric a does not tell students exactly what they must do to complete the test.

Another important point is conciseness. The rubric should not be too long. If the rubric is so long that the student has to take in large amounts of information, then it is likely that he/she may concentrate on what and where to produce their answer rather than on getting the right answer itself. With unnecessarily long rubrics, the objective of measuring the student's true performance, as far as this is possible, will be compromised.

Consider which of the following rubrics is more concise, a or b:

a Read the text which appears on the second page of the text booklet you have been provided with. Look at the answer box which has columns for information. Underneath the heading of each column, you will find spaces in which you should write your answer according to the text. Use the words you hear in the text to fill in each of the columns. Sometimes, you may find that a column has no corresponding information in the text. In these cases, do not write anything in that column. Leave that column blank. All the other columns will require you to write some information.

b Read text number 7 and fill in the information in each column of the box next to the text. Write the exact word used in the text in the appropriate column. If there is no information for any particular column, leave the column blank.

In the above cases, b is more concise than a and has the advantage that students do not have to spend time trying to decipher the meaning of rubric a whilst they are attempting to do the test. One way of avoiding any potential problems can be to put the test rubric in the students' mother tongue. When you are checking the tasks themselves you also need to think about background knowledge. It should be impossible to answer any questions correctly without reading or listening to a text. Students should not be able to use their knowledge of the world or background knowledge of certain subject areas to answer the questions.

Consider the following item, taken from a reading test. Can you answer this question?

When was the Boeing 747 (Jumbo Jet) first built?
a the 1950's   b the 1970's   c the 1990's

Many students may be able to answer this question without referring to the reading text in which the answer appears as a result of their knowledge of the subject area. Therefore, those students who happened to know when the Boeing 747 was built would have an unfavourable advantage over those students who did not happen to know the date.

It is also important to look out for any kind of cultural bias when writing or checking test questions. No items in your test should depend on specific knowledge of certain cultures or customs. The test should not require the student to demonstrate knowledge of a particular culture.

Consider the following item, taken from a reading test:
The Smiths are a typical English working class family and they have their meals at normal times. They have their evening tea when they get back from work.

What time do the Smiths have their evening tea?
a 3pm   b 6pm   c 8pm

This question tests knowledge of customs in Britain, rather than ability to read. You cannot answer the question if you do not know what time people eat and when they normally finish work in Britain.

One of the most important considerations is the content of the test. The test should reflect what the students have been doing in class ie should accurately reflect the syllabus and design of the course in terms of content and format.

For example, when writing a progress test after the first seven units of a course, it would be unwise to base the test on the first two units alone. A test at the end of the course should attempt to reflect the whole course or year as far as possible ie the test should sample as widely and unpredictably as possible from the content of the course, bearing in mind time constraints. Therefore, when you are checking your test it is worth asking yourself how well it reflects what you have been doing with your students.

All items in your test should be also relevant in terms of real world language use. The task which students are expected to perform should correspond as closely as possible to some use of the language in the real world. The key here is to make the task appear to the students as something which they might actually have to do with the language.

> Consider the following item, taken from a writing test. Is this a task that students might have to do in the real world?:
> Composition: Write a short composition (about 250 words) about what you did in your summer holidays. Include details about the journey, the place and the accommodation where you stayed.

Without searching too far for potential relevance, it is difficult to think of a context in the real world when a language learner might need to produce this kind of written work. The same type of production might be elicited in a more authentic manner by setting the written piece in the context of, for example, answering a letter from a penfriend asking about the summer holidays.

Time is also very important and your test should not place undue pressure on the students in terms of time needed to complete the tasks set. In reading tests, students should not be required to answer items in a limited time which would be completely unrealistic for a reader in real life. Time should be allowed to read the text, read the items and answer the items, including a time allowance for re-reading for clarification and possible amendment to answers.

In listening tests, students should not be required to answer too many items in a short period of time, especially if the listening text gives answers to items in rapid succession, perhaps not even giving time to note down required answers.

In writing tests, students should not be required to produce *x* amount of words in an unrealistic time limit, eg a letter to a prospective employer in *5-10* minutes. Time should be given for planning, writing, reading and possible re-writing.

In speaking tests where there is an interlocutor, unrealistic time pressures on answers and oral production should be avoided, eg hurrying students into an answer with no time for reflection or checking understanding or asking for repetition.

Finally, when you are writing your tests you should also take into account practical administrative factors. For example, you should not write tests that require a lot of photocopying if it is difficult and expensive to do in your situation. You should also avoid using equipment (like video recorders) which is difficult for you to obtain.

Checking tests

Look at the test items on the next few pages. Identify the problems in test items.

Use this checklist to help you:

- Is there *more than one possible answer?*
- Is there *no correct answer?*
- Is there *enough context* provided to choose the correct answer?
- Could a *test-wise student guess the answer* without reading or listening to the text?
- Does it *test what it says it is going to test?* (or does it test something else?)
- Does it test the *ability to do puzzles*, or IQ in general, rather than language?
- Does it test students' *imagination* rather than their linguistic ability?
- Does it test students *skills* or *content knowledge* of other academic areas?
- Does it test *general knowledge of the world?*
- Does it test *cultural knowledge* rather than language?
- Are the *rubrics (instructions)* clear and concise? Is the language in the instructions more difficult than that in the text?
- Will it be very *time-consuming* to mark and difficult to work out scores?
- Are there any *typing errors* that make it difficult to do?

Speaking
1 Interviewer: *'Right, now María what do you think about cricket?'*
2 Interviewer: *'Can you tell me the names of the animals in the picture?'*
3 Interviewer: *'What do you think about the political situation in South Africa?'*

Listening
4 Listen to the talk and choose the correct answer:
a All elephants live in Africa.
b Elephants live in South America.
c Elephants live in Africa and India.

5 Listen to the dialogue and answer the questions. You must write complete sentences (remember adverbs of frequency).
Example:
What is the weather like in Sydney in June?
In June it is rainy and sometimes it is cold.

You get three marks for each correct sentence, one mark for each adverb of frequency used and half for each word you use related to weather.

Writing

6 Write a ghost story (200 words). Try to make it dramatic and exciting!

7 Write instructions for a scientific experiment. Draw diagrams to illustrate it.

8 Write a report of an interview with a famous pop star. Use reported statements and questions. Example: I asked him about his family and he told me that...

Reading

9 Read the text below and answer this question: What did the captain hear?

a A sheep or goat.

b A strange noise from the sea.

c Somebody in pain.

It was a dark and misty night. The captain was sleeping in his cabin and everything was quiet. Suddenly, the captain woke up. He heard a strange noise coming from the deck. It sounded like an animal in pain, maybe a sheep or a goat. He got dressed and cautiously climbed the ladder.

10 Complete the sentences with one of these words:

a however

b but

c in spite of

d although

   They continued playing football .... it was raining

Vocabulary

11 What are these words? nsyun / ureufnitr / angroe / dolc

12 Which is the odd one out?

a basketball

b table tennis

c ice-hockey

d cricket

Grammar

13 Complete the sentence with 'will' or 'going to':

   Tomorrow I think it..................rain.

14 Choose the alternative that is closest in meaning to the word which is underlined:

   I've just finished it.

a A minute ago.

b Yesterday.

c A week ago.

15 Marking scheme: Exercise A:

   1 = 2.5   2 = 2   3 = 3.25   4 =1.75   5 = 2   6 = .5   TOTAL = 12

Administering tests

As we pointed out in the introduction to this book, being tested as a student and testing learners as a teacher can be traumatic. Therefore we need to do what we can to reduce tension. At the same time, we need to make sure that formal assessment does take place under test conditions ie that students cannot copy or help each other. In normal classroom conditions we want to encourage co-operation, but when carrying out formal assessment we need to do the opposite, to make sure that we are testing the performance of each individual learner. We thus need to reduce to a minimum any cheating that might go on in our classroom.

The first thing to consider is the place. Most of the time we give our tests in our own classrooms. Before giving out the test papers it is a good idea to try to separate students as much as possible, by moving desks or placing students around the room. If it is impossible to do this it may be worth trying to move to another room. If you do this, it is worth choosing a place where there will be a minimum of interruptions and outside background noise.

Time also has to be considered. Firstly, you should tell students how long they have at the beginning as well as writing it on the paper. In your own classroom tests you can be relatively flexible and give students a bit longer if you see that they are having problems. If it is a school test it is more important to avoid any unfair advantage for some students who might benefit from more time.

It is important to have materials well prepared in advance. Make sure that before you administer the test you have all the necessary printed material and that there are adequate supplies of all test papers, maps, charts or any other printed matter for the number of students who will be taking the test. Make sure that photocopying is of a satisfactory quality and that no errors have been made in printing and preparation. If there are any errors, eg spelling, repeated questions, inform students before the test begins.

In addition, make sure that you have checked any recorded material before the test is to be administered. Sometimes, you may find that there is nothing you can do about a certain problem, eg poor quality of recording or varying sound recording levels. In these cases, students should simply be warned. However, all attempts should be made to remedy the problem before the next administration of the test. Electrical equipment also needs to be checked beforehand. Make sure that any audio equipment is adequate in terms of sound quality and acoustics in the room where the test is to be administered.

Your students will need to be prepared for the test. If you have short and regular progress tests they will be much less worried than if they have fewer but more important tests. Tell students in advance that you will be giving them a test and at what time they are expected to arrive, what time the test will start and what time the test will finish. Students should also know what materials they need to bring with them to the test, eg pens, pencils, erasers etc. If dictionaries are to be used in any test, students should be told to bring their own copy of preferably the same edition so that no student has an unfair advantage.

Tell students about the test conditions. For example, there should be no talking and if they wish to ask a question they should raise their hand. Students should also be seated in a way that they cannot copy answers from a neighbour or communicate answers to a neighbour. You can also tell them what will happen if they are caught cheating, for example, they might be given a zero score or even disciplinary action might be taken.

If you are administering a test with your colleagues you need to agree on conditions. Decisions should be taken beforehand about what to do in cases of students arriving late, students copying, students finishing before the allocated time etc. Many of these decisions will differ from institution to institution and may depend on policy and internal rules and regulations. If you or your colleagues are to act as interlocutors in speaking tests, it is essential that everybody agrees on how to act as interlocutor and what is to be expected of students in the test. All those who are to act as interlocutors should hold meetings before the test to agree on criteria for performance and to practise using the test materials.

Marking tests

Marking is one of the most time-consuming parts of many teachers' jobs. As we suggested earlier (in the sub-section on planning assessment programmes), short and regular assessment tasks spread the test marking load over the whole term. This not only avoids stress and exhaustion on your part, but it should also mean that you will be able to mark more accurately and reliably. We have also mentioned the need to consider marking time when choosing test formats. With very small classes we can afford to have more labour-intensive test formats (for example open compositions and oral interviews). If we have very large classes we will need to choose formats that will enable us to mark large numbers of tests in a short period of time (like multiple choice questions).

On the one hand we have *discrete item* or *objective tests*. These tests are so called because of the way they are marked. An objective test could in theory be marked by any person capable of interpreting and applying a marking key which gives the correct answers which are unique and not negotiable. An example would be a template or mask as often used to mark multiple-choice questions. For example, the only possible answer to question 6 is (b)option. The person marking the test will simply apply the template or marking key and will be able to total the correct answers which will give a raw score. In this sense, objective testing can be considered as marking by counting.

Objective tests are easily and quickly marked by non-specialists. However, they can be difficult to write so that they are reliable, eg in the case of the multiple-choice question paper it is often difficult to devise suitable and plausible distracters and the guessing factor is also very high. Another disadvantage is in the case where many variants of a similar answer would be a suitable and correct answer to an item. For example in a listening test, what is an acceptable answer to the question *'What does the man want?'* The answer key might state that the correct answer is *'He wants to buy petrol'*. But would *'Buy petrol'*, or *'Petrol – buy'* or *'petrol'* also be acceptable answers? This would depend on the test designer, who would be responsible for ensuring that answer keys contained all possible answers.

Subjective tests, as opposed to objective tests, are not based on counting, but depend on somebody's opinion, a judgement, a decision about candidate performance. The person who is to make the judgement is expected to be qualified to make that judgement, eg you as a language teacher could make judgements about oral performances of students in a speaking test. On the other hand, many of the people who may be perfectly qualified to mark your objective, multiple-choice listening test may not be suitable for use as raters of oral performance. *Subjective tests* can provide a wide sample of students' language in a relatively short time – think of how much your students could actually say in 15 minutes.

They can be objectivised by using rating scales which outline a description of what each point on a scale means, eg 5 = the ability to … . *Subjective tests* may take up a lot of your time. For example, if a class of forty students can be tested at the same time using a forty minute reading test, this is much more practical in terms of time than holding forty interviews of fifteen minutes each or marking forty written compositions.

Reliability of raters is the greatest problem area. The key question is how to ensure that different raters apply the scales in the same way. This is called inter-rater reliability. Also, another question is how to ensure that the same rater will apply the scales in the same way on different days or at different times of the day. This is called intra-rater reliability. These issues can be addressed by rating workshops and training packages, although this implies more time spent by teachers and any other person expected to carry out rating of tests.

It must be pointed out here that objectively marked tests are not to be considered as good and subjectively marked tests as bad. They are simply different ways of marking.

When you are marking a test that you have written yourself it is a good idea to define beforehand the answer key especially when other teachers are going to mark the test. The key should be easy to use and leave no doubt in the marker's mind as to what is a correct and incorrect answer. This can be a relatively simple process in the case of multiple-choice items or rather more complicated in the case of open-ended questions. With open-ended questions, ensure that the answer key covers all possible answers. After producing your answer key, it is a good idea to show it to a colleague if possible. Your colleague could check the answers for possible errors, additions or deletions to be made. After that, you should agree on the answer key with all those who will be using it to mark the test.

It is also a good idea to work out how you are going to distribute marks before administering the test. It can be very useful to write the marking scheme on the test paper itself, so that the students also know how much each section is worth.

When other teachers are going to use the test you will need to produce a marking scheme. The marking scheme should be easy to use and should leave no doubt in the marker's mind as to how many points each item is worth. Markers should not be expected to perform complicated mathematical calculations to arrive at a student's final score. Look at the example of a marking key on page 48.

Subjective tests and rating

For subjective tests we need to look at rating ie where results are based on somebody's opinion about candidate performance, eg in an oral test or a written composition. We looked at the subject in the chapter on informal assessment (particularly in the sub-chapters on speaking and writing). However, for formal tests it is not only important to establish criteria. If more than one teacher is administering the test, we will need to agree on interpretation of rating criteria.

We have already mentioned the two kinds of rating scales which we can use. Rating scales can either contain descriptions of all activities within one level or can break down the activities into separate scales and provide descriptions for each activity at each level. The first is holistic rating and the second example is called analytic rating (see page 13).

The advantage of holistic rating for testing is that raters can internalise the descriptions in a relatively short period of time, eg after practice with a few sample performances. This system is therefore practical and quick to administer. The disadvantage is that student performances can often cut across the descriptions, eg one activity may belong to level 3 and another activity to level 4. However, raters are trained in all cases to choose the closest description of the performance.

The advantage of analytic rating is that raters may find it easier to assign a certain level using simplified and discrete scales. The disadvantage is that it will probably be less practical than holistic rating in terms of time, paper and training.

Look at page 46 for an example of oral rating scales.

When you are assessing your students in this way, it is important to achieve *intra-rater reliability* – to make sure that you rate them consistently. In an attempt to increase our own *intra-rater reliability* we can look at a piece of students' work and then look at it again two weeks later. Then we can compare assessments and if there are differences, think about why and where we went wrong.

An important factor when more than one teacher is marking a test is *inter-rater reliability* – to ensure that all raters assess in the same way and that all raters agree on the interpretation and meaning of the descriptions in the rating scales. The objective is to minimise the possibility of a student's mark being affected by the rater who assesses their performance.

In an attempt to maximise *inter-rater reliability*, you could hold meetings with your colleagues to discuss rating scales and samples of student performances could be provided. Raters could discuss the sample performances, rate them, and thus see if they are applying the same criteria. Written performances should be easy to supply. In the case of oral performances, these could be recorded on audio or video tape.

Inter-rater reliability activity
Written performance

- Look at the example of the writing assessment task on page 39.
- Then look at the criteria for marking it on page 39.
- Give copies of three answers on page 58 to one or more of your colleagues. Also give them a copy of the marking criteria.
- Read the letters yourself and rate them.
- Ask your colleague(s) to use the marking criteria to rate the performances.
- Compare your results and if there are any discrepancies, discuss the performances and the rating scales. Try to come to an agreement about your rating of the compositions. Then compare your marks with those on page 62.
- The next time you are marking written performance from a test, do the same activity with your colleagues.

Dear ~~Robdney~~

I'am Elena. I'am 13 years old I live in Madrid with my family I have two ~~brothers~~, chena y Antonio chena ~~has~~ ~~12 years~~ is 12 years old and Antonio is 12 years old. My hobbies are play tennis ~~and I like to sing~~

I'am Elena. I'am 13 years old. I've two brothers My mother teacher and my father is teacher. We live on Madrid I've ~~th~~ 3 hobbies, ~~I I like to~~ I watch ~~of~~ the tv. I listen music and I sing (very bad) but very bad ~~I don't like~~ my favourite sports is the tennis My ~~favou~~ ~~Favourite~~ ~~mus~~ Favourite ~~singer~~ group music is Rem' I go to the school ~~the~~ school is near of my house. I hate the school and I hate the Fish I collect rubbers the class of history is very boring.

44 Galileo 4°F
Spain 28080 Madrid
10 March.

Dear Rodney

Hi!. My name's Marta. I am 12 years old. I have got ~~one~~ a sister her name is Pilar. ~~I have got~~ ~~My mother's~~ ~~the Name's of my mother~~ the name of my mother is M. Asunaon and the name of ~~of~~ my father is Roque.

I live in Madrid ~~and~~ I like Madrid My hobbies are play basketball and collect stamps. I like basketball and I ~~look~~ see every day

I like music My favourite music is ~~pop and rock~~. ~~My favourite group~~ My favourite groups are Mecano and Roxete. Also I like maquina and bacalas ~~I like~~ Write to me and tell me things

Bye
Marta

30 Gorri Road
Madrid SPAIN
10.3.93

Dear Rodney

Hello! My name is Henry and I'm your new penfriend I'm fourteen years old. I haven't got sisters or brothers My dad is called Jose My mum's called Merche and she works in an office. I live with my parents and with my grandmother in Madrid. Madrid is the best town! It's beautiful It isn't boring. I've got lots of hobbies. I collect foreing coins. I have coins from India, Corea, Japan, Nepal, U.SA, Singapur and I have coins from lots of countries too.

I would like to play in REAL MADRID I like the sports in general. Football is my favourite sport. I play football in my school with my friends. I also like basketball, table tennis, tennis etc I don't like heavy metal music.

Bye
Henry.

By doing activities like these, you will achieve a much greater degree of reliability for tests at your school. You will also need to work out criteria that is clear for both you and your colleagues.

Inter/intra-rater reliability activity
- Look at the example of a paired oral test on page 45.
- Give the test to students in your class and record some of the discussions onto audio tape. Make sure that the tapes are labelled with student names. (You might want to use numbers rather than names for increased reliability of the activity !)
- Assess the student performances using the rating scales given on page 46 and keep a record of the marks assigned.

Inter-rater reliability
- Arrange a meeting with one or more of your colleagues and explain that you want to see if you can agree on the level of student performances and whether the rating scales are easy to use.
- Give your colleague(s) the oral test material and the rating scales and give them time to familiarise themselves with the task.
- Play a selection of student performances (perhaps 3 or 4) including, if possible, what in your opinion is a clear pass, a clear fail and a borderline case.
- Ask your colleague(s) to use the rating scales to rate the performances using the rating scales.
- Compare your original results and if there are discrepancies, discuss the performances and the rating scales. Try to come to an agreement on the criteria to be used for each descriptor in the rating scales. (Don't worry if there are minor differences in rating – these are to be expected).

Intra-rater reliability
- Keep the recordings and original marks in a safe place and, if you have time, set aside an hour or so one day about two or three weeks after you administered the oral test.
- Play the recordings again and rate the performances again, in a random order, using the same rating scales. Do not refer to the original marks.
- When you have finished, compare your new ratings with the original marks.
- If the marks are the same, you appear to be quite a reliable rater within your own performance ! If the marks are a little different, don't worry – this might be expected. If the marks are very different, think about reasons why this might be so – are you stricter or more lenient? Do you think that perhaps the rating scales are confusing? How could the problem be solved?

2.5 Results from formal assessment

Once students have taken a formal test and it has been marked, you will have results. These results will usually give a mark or score for each student, for example *68* out of *100*. On the other hand, the results might simply tell you that a student has passed or failed the test. But what is a pass mark? What is a fail?

One way of deciding this is by *norm-referencing*. This consists of putting the students in a list or scale depending on the mark they achieved in the test. The student with the lowest mark is at the bottom of the list and the student with the highest mark is at the top of the list. All other students are between the two extremes. A pass in the test might be decided as the top *60%* of students, with *40%* failing, or as the top *50%* of students with *50%* failing. This is often used in public examinations, but it is not suitable for classroom situations. For example, it might create a situation in which a high ability candidate fails because the other students in the same class are of a higher ability. Conversely, it might create a situation in which a low ability candidate passes because the other candidates in the class are of a lower ability. The extremes might be that student *X* achieves *90%* in the test and fails because all other students achieved between *91* and *100%* ; or student *Y* achieves *35%* in the test and passes because all other students achieved between *1* and *34%*.

Criterion-referencing is a much more suitable way of making decisions about classroom tests. This consists of making decisions about what is a pass and what is a fail before the results are obtained. It normally means that we define certain criteria that candidates in the test must conform to, eg if the candidate can do *X*, *Y* and *Z*, then he/she passes – if he/she cannot do *X*, *Y* and *Z*, then he/she fails the test. An example is the driving test in the United Kingdom: there is a specified list of things which the candidate must be able to do in order to pass the test, eg make an emergency stop, turn the car round in the road in a number of manoeuvres, reverse round a corner etc. It can be a fair way of interpreting results because a pass or fail is decided on each candidate's performance in the test irrespective of the rest of the candidates who take the same test. Also, candidates know that they are not in competition with the rest of those who take the test.

Finally, when we have interpreted the results of our tests and decided which students have passed and failed, we need to go over tests with students. It is important to go over the answers to progress tests with the whole class, so that students realise where they went wrong. Students can then think about what they need to do to do to get better results the next time. When you give back pieces of writing done under test conditions you can use correction codes in the way suggested in the previous section (Informal assessment – writing). When you give students their results on oral tests it is also important to identify what their strong and weak points are.

In this way results from formal tests can feed into learning and give students (as well as you the teacher) vital information about both performance and progress.

Summary

In conclusion, the following key points should be remembered when administering formal tests and implementing a formal assessment programme.

◆ There are many reasons why we should test our students and formal tests should not be discarded as a waste of valuable time. On the contrary, they should be seen as time well spent in helping to form an accurate assessment of our students' ability.

◆ A formal assessment programme needs to be carefully planned and should tie in with your educational objectives and the extent and timing of other forms of measuring students' ability such as self and informal assessment.

◆ There are many different types of test and test formats. Each one is useful in its own context and is less useful in other contexts. Much will depend on what you want the test to do for you in your teaching situation.

◆ Writing, marking and administering tests may appear to be a relatively simple matter. However, the extent to which these are carried out successfully will affect the success of your tests and ultimately the reliability of the results you obtain. This in turn will directly affect the decisions you make about your students – our aim must be to make decisions which are based on accurate and reliable information.

Suggested answers to practical activities where necessary

Washback effects

1 Bad washback. Students will feel that luck was more important than hard work.
2 Bad washback. Students will feel that classwork has been a waste of time.
3 Good washback. The information will help you plan your course to suit the needs of your students.
4 Good washback. Students will feel they have been tested fairly.

Your testing

a = placement
b = progress
c = diagnostic
d = summative
e = proficiency

Identifying test formats

Assessment task 1: Combined (reading/writing)
Assessment task 2: Guided writing (notes and pictures)
Assessment task 3:
1 Identifying topic (matching)
2 Table completion.
3 Short answer questions.
Assessment task 4:
a True/false   b Short answer questions
Assessment task 5:
1 Information gap (real information)
2 Picture description
3 Roleplay
Assessment task 6:
Roleplay
Assessment task 7:
a Gap-fill   b Cued questions (from answers)   c Editing
d Cued vocabulary (pictures)

Checking tests

1 Cultural knowledge that ss could not be expected to know.
2 Content knowledge. Also more of a vocabulary test than a speaking test which it purports to be (therefore low validity).
3 General knowledge of the world- which ss cannot be expected to know (particularly young students).
4 You know the answer without listening. (c)
5 Doesn't test listening but is a test of language.
6 Tests students' imagination more than their English.
7 Tests content knowledge of science.
8 Is a language test rather than a test of writing (to communicate).
9 No answer is possible here.
10 This is a test of language not of reading.
11 This anagram activity tests the ability to do puzzles not knowledge of vocab.
12 More than one answer is possible here, (eg basketball = no bat/cricket = played outside)
13 Not enough context is provided here, either is possible.
14 Not enough context is provided. All three are possible.
15 The marking scheme is horribly complex and will waste a lot of time.

Inter-rater reliability for written performance
Suggested marks for letters

1 **4** The letter is badly organised. Because of this and because of the large number of very basic structural and lexical errors, it is very difficult to read and understand. Another factor which makes understanding difficult is the handwriting and constant crossing out of words.

2 **6** In this letter there is some real communication. If this were a real penfriend letter, the person getting it would learn something about Marta. However, there are quite a few mistakes and crossings out which makes it difficult to follow in parts.

3 **9** This letter communicates the information needed reasonably clearly and with only a few mistakes of spelling or grammar. Finally, the letter is enthusiastic and interesting to read.

Action points: formal assessment

1 As a result of reading this chapter are you going to make any changes in the way you test your students? If so, what are they?

2 Are you going to give all your formal tests in one block, or are you going to spread them out over the term?
(*For example*, using shorter assessment tasks)

3 What kind of weighting are you going to give to different skills and language?
(*For example*, 30% speaking / 20% writing etc)

4 What kind of test formats are you going to use?
(*For example*, multiple-choice, guided writing etc)

5 The next time you have to write tests are you going to do it on your own or with a group of colleagues?

6 How are you going to administer your tests? What test conditions are you going to introduce? How are you going to try to reduce anxiety amongst your students?

7 How are you going to mark your tests? What measures are you going to take to increase the reliability of your marking?

8 What proportion of marks are you going to get from formal as opposed to other forms of assessment?

---

3 Self-assessment

3.1 Introduction to self-assessment

We have looked at how we can assess our students, informally through assessing class and homework or formally through tests or assessment tasks. If both these types of assessment are done thoroughly, we will probably get a fair picture of our students' problems and a reasonably accurate measure of their progress. However, we are ignoring an extremely useful source of information, the students themselves. *Self-assessment* can provide us with useful information about students' expectations and needs, their problems and worries, how they feel about their own progress, their reactions to the materials and methods being used, what they think about the course in general. Self-assessment can also be a much more direct and efficient way of getting information than teacher assessment. For example, rather than give a comprehensive diagnostic test to find out what areas of language students are weak on, it is much quicker to ask students directly what problems they feel they have.

The most important benefits of self-assessment are related to its impact on learning. Self-assessment is an integral part of learning. To learn anything we need to assess what we know already and how we can improve. We normally do this subconsciously. If we are learning to cook, we learn by thinking about what we have done and then improving on it in the future.

Thinking about your language learning

Look at 1–12 below. Tick (✓) the points which you have thought about and put a cross (✗) next to those you have never considered.

1 your *performance* in another language in a particular situation, eg speaking with somebody at a party
2 the fact that on some days you can *communicate* well and on other days you can't say anything
3 why you can *understand* people in some situations but not in others, eg you can understand people when you are talking face to face, but not on the telephone
4 why some people are easy for you to *understand* and others aren't
5 which common *mistakes* you keep on making, eg grammar/vocab/pron
6 which *grammatical* areas are difficult for you
7 which *sounds* are difficult for you to say
8 what new *words* it would be useful for you to learn
9 *how much* you have learnt in a lesson or over a week
10 how much progress you have made over a *course of study*
11 which of these areas you need to *improve* on most: listening speaking reading writing grammar pronunciation
12 how you can *practise* and improve on your own

Your answers

If you have placed a tick next to most of the questions on page 63, you have been thinking about your learning and assessing yourself. You probably did this on your own, outside the language class. Do you think it would have been helpful to have had guidance and encouragement in assessing yourself?

Give the same questionnaire to your students (translate it into their L1 if necessary). This questionnaire can be useful to start your students thinking about their own learning and realising the importance of self-assessment.

Self-assessment is thus a vital part of the learning process. If we rely totally on teacher-based assessment, we are only carrying out part of the job of assessment. We are diagnosing problems and we are measuring the progress that our students have made. This information can feed back into our own teaching, but it does not necessarily feed back into the learning process. Students are often passive and wait for us to tell them if they have done well or badly. At no time do they need to think about what they have done, and why they have done well or badly. This can be seen clearly with writing. When students are given back corrected compositions they often just look at the mark and do not really learn from the feedback.

There is a saying in English that *'you learn from your own mistakes'*. Perhaps we could qualify this to *'you learn from your own mistakes when you think about them'*. By conscious self-assessment, students are involved in the process of assessment and therefore the information from it can feed back into their own learning. Self-assessment helps learners to think about their own progress and problems and then to find ways of changing, adapting and improving. This can be seen with the example mentioned earlier of writing. If students are encouraged to assess their own work, to think about their own mistakes and to try to correct them, they are more likely to improve than when only the teacher assesses and corrects.

Teacher assessment

teacher assessment
of learner's progress

conclusions about progress
diagnosis of problems

teaching:
course content

Teacher and learner assessment

teacher/learner assessment

conclusions about progress
diagnosis of problems

learning:
course content

teaching:
course content

In the teaching-based model above, the results from assessment do feed back into the content of a course. Remedial work is done when necessary and objectives can be changed as a result of information from assessment. However, learners never need to think consciously about their own problems. In the learning-based model both the teacher's assessment and students' self-assessment have a direct effect on the learning process.

While there are many benefits to be derived from self-assessment, many teachers may have serious reservations about implementing it. Firstly, it can take up a lot of time, which is at a premium in most classes. This means that it must be streamlined and integrated with other classroom activities. Secondly, self-assessment implies a knowledge about language and learning which most secondary learners do not have. Therefore, self-assessment can only work if it is accompanied by learner training. Thirdly, many teachers may have their doubts about the maturity of students when they are asked to give themselves a mark, which will be taken into account in their overall assessment. The tendency to give themselves a higher mark could make self-assessment an unreliable influence on assessment. In fact many students tend to do the opposite and give themselves a lower mark than they deserve. In either case the link between assessment and other areas of assessment needs to be looked at closely.

Perhaps the most important thing about self-assessment is that it cannot work in a context where marks have an intrinsic value in themselves and there is competition between students. In fact most self-assessment should have nothing at all to do with marks. It should concentrate on thinking about performance and progress in individual terms. This is particularly so in mixed ability classes where consideration of learners' progress has to take into account the often very different starting points of individuals.

In this chapter we will look at laying the foundations for self-assessment, starting from the first week of a course. Then we will look at how self-assessment of performance can be integrated into classroom activities throughout a course. After that we will look at how students can review their own progress systematically and at the link between self-assessment and other kinds of assessment.

Before we look in detail at how to implement self-assessment in the classroom let us look at some of the techniques that we have at our disposal. Many of these are similar to those looked at in previous sections on teacher assessment. The difference is that in this case the students themselves carry out the assessment.

Techniques for self-assessment

Look at the techniques below. Have you ever used any of them yourself? Which would you like to try out with your students?

Descriptions
- Profiles
  students write reports about their English and give them to you.
- Learner diaries
  students keep learner diaries:
  records of what they have done in class
  what they have learnt
  what problems they have had
- Counselling sessions
  you talk to students individually about their own progress

Rating
- Rating scales
  students rate their own performance or progress using a rating scale with descriptors, eg a scale of 1 to 5. Students can use this structure with no problems at all. Peer rating of other students can also give students practice at this.
- General rating
  students give themselves an 'impression' mark for different areas, eg writing/speaking
- Graphs
  students rate how much they have understood using a graph
- Adjectives
  students choose from lists of adjectives to describe their own attitudes, eg hard-working/relaxed/lazy

Monitoring
- Self-editing
  students look through their own compositions and try to correct their mistakes. Peer editing can also give them practice at the same time as helping their partners
- Correction codes
  students use your correction code, eg Pr= preposition, to try to correct their own mistakes
- Taping
  students listen to a recording of themselves and try to correct mistakes
- Grading mistakes
  students grade mistakes in order of seriousness
- Test yourself
  (self-check) students do short tests to find out how much they know

Questionnaires

- Listing
  students list specific problems for them, like words that they have difficulty pronouncing
- Ranking preferences
  students rank activities in terms of which they enjoy, eg 1= listening to songs 2= watching video
- Ranking problems
  students rank areas that are difficult for them, eg grammar: modal verbs
- Multiple choice questions
  students answer questions about their habits, eg How much do you study?
  a a lot
  b quite a lot
  c a little
  d not at all
- Agreeing/disagreeing
  students agree or disagree with statements about learning, eg
  Learning is easy. They could use a range of statements from easy to difficult.
- Can/cannot questions
  students answer questions about what they can or cannot do, eg Can you talk about the weather?
- Short answer questions
  students answer questions about their preferences, performance or progress, eg What topic areas would you like to look at this year?

Surveys

- Group surveys
  students find out about each other's learning preferences or problems and then report the group results to the rest of the class.
- Class surveys
  students go around the class and ask questions about learning to the others. Then they report the results to the whole class.

3.2 Laying the foundations

The best time to start integrating self-assessment into a course and to introduce students to self-assessment is from the first day of class. Before you open a textbook or begin to do other classroom activities, you have the ideal opportunity to get students to think about their own learning. The best way of doing this can be either through learner questionnaires or through classroom survey activities. In this section we will look at some learner training activities for the first two weeks of term in which self-assessment features prominently.

Classroom survey: past learning experiences

Even if students come from similar learning backgrounds it can be useful to get them to recall previous learning experiences. As well as reminding students of their past learning experiences the feedback from students can give you useful information to help your own planning.

Learner questionnaire: Initial self-assessment

A simple questionnaire can help you find out in more detail about how your students feel about their own English, doing an initial self-assessment of strong and weak areas. It is important to realise that at this stage any grades that students give are totally subjective and related to how they feel about previous learning experiences. These questionnaires can be handed in individually, in which case they can provide a useful initial record of each student's feelings towards their learning. Another way of gathering this sort of feedback from older and higher level learners is through a letter or note directed to you the teacher. Students can write a note telling you about their problems and how they feel about the different areas of English.

Give this questionnaire to your students at the beginning of the year.

My Learning

a So far have you found learning English:
  * quite difficult?
  * quite easy?
  * very difficult?
b Which of these areas of English are easiest for you? Order them in these terms (1 = easiest 7 = the most difficult)
  * speaking
  * listening
  * writing
  * reading
  * grammar
  * vocabulary
  * pronunciation
c Give yourself a mark out of ten for each of the areas above.
Example:
speaking 6/10

Don't worry about other people, think about how you feel about the different areas. If you feel satisfied, give yourself a good mark; if you don't give yourself a low mark.

Diagnostic questionnaires

If your students come from a variety of primary schools, it can be interesting to find out what they have covered and to ask students what they think they are able to do. By collecting them in and looking at them you can get a better idea of your students. At the same time the students themselves are receiving training in self-assessment.

Look through this diagnostic questionnaire and modify it according to the needs of your students (putting it into their L1 if necessary). Then give it to your students at the beginning of the year. You can also include other areas, eg listening: How well students can understand different people in different situations.

What can I do in English?

Mark which of the things below you can do like this:

a I can do this well

b I can do it

c I can't do it

- Ask the teacher for help, eg about the meaning of a word
- Ask the teacher for permission to do things, eg open the window
- Say my name, address and telephone number.
- Talk about what I like, eg music/hobbies
- Talk about my family.
- Tell the time.
- Buy things in a shop.
- Ask information about prices/times of trains or buses.
- Describe people and animals.
- Talk about what I do every day.
- Talk about the weather.
- Give and ask for directions.
- Talk about what I did last weekend.
- Talk about my last holidays.
- Talk about my life in the past.
- Give my opinions about films/TV/sport.
- Give instructions.
- Make suggestions to do things with friends.
- Invite people to parties.
- Agree and disagree with people.

Establishing objectives and goals

Having thought about past learning experiences that students have had, it is a good time to think about objectives for the coming year. While this can also be done unit by unit, the start of a course is a good time for learners to think about their priorities and needs. At the end of the course they will then be able to refer back to them to assess whether they have reached them or not. In this way awareness of initial goals is an important step in the development of self-assessment.

The degree of learner participation in establishing objectives will depend on your teaching situation. In many secondary situations, the overall objectives will already have been established (by the ministry or the school department). However, this does not mean that students cannot be consulted about objectives and given the chance to think about their own needs. Again this is particularly important in mixed ability situations and where students can have the opportunity of working on their own or in small groups.

Having consulted students at the beginning of the year, their needs can be taken into account in course planning throughout the year. For example, if you find that students are particularly interested in a certain topic it may be possible to relate a task-based unit or project to it.

Setting objectives

Give your students a list with some of your objectives for the coming year. Tell them individually to choose five priorities for themselves (eg listening to stories/speaking about likes). If they like they can add other objectives (particularly in terms of topic areas to cover).
They can hand these in to you individually or discuss their answers in groups and then report them back to the rest of the class.

Objectives (elementary level)
- Topic areas
  nature and the environment, shopping, food
- Speaking
  using English in the classroom
  talking about your own lives – likes, homes, food
- Listening
  getting used to listening without understanding everything
  listening to stories, conversations, cartoons
- Reading
  getting used to understanding the general idea
  reading teenage magazines, comics, simplified readers using dictionaries
- Writing
  planning and organising writing
  writing postcards, penfriend letters
- Grammar
  revision and introduction of basic tenses: present simple
  present continuous, past simple, future
- Vocabulary
  related to: classroom, animals, food
- Pronunciation
  difficult sounds
- Learning
  organising vocabulary, books, self-assessment

As well as looking at overall course objectives, the objectives of particular modules or units can be looked at throughout the course. Before beginning a new module you can inform students of the most important aims and encourage them to think about which are most useful to them. Then, when students have finished the module they will be able to look back and decide to what degree the objectives have been achieved.

Learning skills

The beginning of a course is also a good time for students to assess how effective they are as learners and from there to think about how they could become better learners. This involves thinking about both their attitudes towards learning and their study habits.

Self-assessment of learning style

Look through the questionnaire below. Think about how you might adapt it for your own students (translating it into their L1 if necessary). Having given it to your students you can discuss the answers.

Are you a good learner?
1 What is your attitude towards other countries?
a I'm very interested in how other people live.
b I'm quite interested in how other people live.
c I'm only interested in where I live.
2 What is your attitude towards English?
a I'm interested in listening to songs in English and watching films and TV programmes in English.
b I only like songs and films from my own country.
3 For which of these things do you think English may be useful?
a For travelling to different countries.
b For helping to get me a job.
c For studying (at school or university).
4 Do you try to speak English in class?
a Always.
b Sometimes.
c Never.
5 What do you bring to class?
a My coursebook, vocabulary book and a notebook.
b Only my coursebook.
c Nothing.
6 What do you do when you find an important new word?
a I write it down on a piece of paper.
b I don't write it down, I say it to myself.
c I write it in my vocabulary book.

7 **When you are listening to the cassette in class and you only understand a little, how do you feel?**
   a Fine. I know that some listenings are more difficult than others, I try to understand as much as I can.
   b A bit frustrated but I continue listening.
   c Very depressed. I stop listening.

8 **When your are reading, which of these things do you do?**
   a If I see a new word I try to guess the meaning from the context. If I cannot and the word is important, I use my dictionary.
   b I ask the teacher what it means.
   c I stop reading.

9 **When you get written work back from the teacher, what do you do?**
   a Look at the mistakes I have made and think about how I can improve next time.
   b I look through it quickly.
   c I only look at the mark, then I throw it away.

10 **Which of these things do you try to do outside the class?**
   a Listen to songs in English.
   b Read stories in English.
   c Speak in English when I meet foreign people.
   d Watch films or TV in English.
   e Think about any English words I see on advertisements and labels.

One point to remember when students are assessing their own attitudes and learning habits is that there is not always a 'correct' answer. For different learners different learning strategies can be effective. For example, if you are considering how students learn vocabulary best you will find that some strategies (like using word networks or drawing pictures) are suited to some learners but not to others. What is important is for students to assess how effective they are as learners and if there are any ways in which they can become more effective.

Learner diaries

Another important step at this stage is to establish one of the most important instruments in self-assessment, *the learner diary*. Learner diaries are records by students of what has happened in their language learning over a period of time (for instance a lesson or a week). They can be very detailed and include a lot of information, such as what went on in class, what students feel they have learned, what problems they have had and what they are going to do to overcome them. Complex diaries are however somewhat impractical for most secondary school learners, mainly due to restrictions of time. A complex diary could take up the majority of class time in many situations. Therefore, it is perhaps better for diaries to be simple and short, so that they can be filled in during a spare five or ten minutes at the end of a class. In this simple form, students can be asked to list the activities they enjoyed and the problems that they had. In this way, students are given a rough record of the week's classes that they can refer to when thinking about their own progress.

Look at the two learner diaries. Which one is most suitable for your learners?

- **Simple learner diary**
  Complete your learner diary every week.
  Example:
  Week 1
  Favourite activities – animal guessing game / animal crossword
  Problems – listening to animal descriptions / new vocabulary – animals
  Week 2
  Favourite activities-
  Problems-
  Week 3
  Favourite activities-
  Problems-

- **Detailed learner diary**
  Answer these questions about the lesson:
- What have I done? (list the activities)
- Which activities were most useful to me?
- Which activities were not so useful for me?
- Did I participate in the lesson?
- Did I work well with my group?
- What did I learn?
- What problems did I have?

All of the activities that we have looked at in this section, as well as providing general learner training, aim to make students reflect on their own learning and to start to assess themselves. The amount of time you spend on these awareness activities will depend on the time you have available. However, even one or two classes focusing on learning and building up mechanisms for future self-assessment like learner diaries, will help students to assess themselves throughout the course and it is important to remember that, if we want our students to take some responsibility for their own learning, we have to make it clear from the beginning.

3.3 Assessing performance

Having established the foundations for self-assessment in the early part of the course, self-assessment then needs to be integrated into day to day classroom activities. The assessment of students' own performance should become an integral part of communicative activities. In this way learners continually keep track of their progress and think about how they can improve in the future.

Self-assessment can also give the teacher feedback about performance without having to correct every single activity done in the classroom. There are many occasions when students can get as much from correcting or assessing their own or each other's work, than from feedback from the teacher.and when we do correct and assess our students' work, it is important that we make the most of the feedback we are giving by getting students to think about their performance as well.

Reading and listening

Before we ask students to assess their own performance in reading and listening, it is useful to do learner training activities to make them aware of different types of reading and listening. It is vital for students to realise that often they do not have to understand everything to do a reading or listening task. They also need to be aware that some texts are much more difficult than others. If they do not realise this and only see progress in a purely linear way, learners can become very frustrated.

For both reading and listening, useful awareness activities are those in which students grade text types according to difficulty or think about different types of reading and listening, how much of a text they need to understand to do a task. Here it can be useful to get students to think about reading and listening in their own language as well.

Learner training (reading)

Think about these three learner training activities yourself. Then try them out with your students in students' L1 if necessary. Tell students to think about reading in their language and in English.

1 Rank these reading texts in order of difficulty:
- postcards from friends
- newspaper articles about politics
- comic strips
- extracts from children's fiction
- encyclopaedia extracts
- magazine articles about people
- notices
- instructions for machines
- travel brochures
- letters from friends

2 How much of a text do you need to understand to do the things below? (eg 1 = 25%)

100% = all of it   75% = most of it   50% = the general idea
25% = some of it

- Find out the main stories in a newspaper.
- Read a comic story for pleasure.
- Follow instructions to assemble a machine.
- Get a fact from an encyclopaedia article.
- Get an idea of what a magazine is like by flicking through it.
- Read a holiday brochure and choose a holiday.

Likewise for listening it is useful for students to think about some of the variables that can affect understanding such as accent, background noise, visual clues and number of speakers. And as with reading it is useful to think about how much we need to understand when we are doing different kinds of listening.

Learner training (listening)

Look at the learner training activity for reading and produce a similar activity for listening.

- Ranking different listening situations (eg listening to your teacher telling a story / listening to a conversation between three native speakers).
- Working out how much you need to understand to do different things (eg listening to find the main points of the news = 50%).

When students are actually doing reading or listening tasks, the most obvious way of assessing performance is by assessing completion of the task. For most tasks this means working out how many correct answers the student gave and why the answers are right and wrong. Students can either do this through self-correction themselves or other students can correct their answers. They can then keep a record of their own results, possibly in their learner diaries.

If these marks carry weight in overall assessment, this procedure is not totally reliable as students could be tempted to cheat. However, if this is not the case, students have no need to mislead you about their own results. Answers can be gone over with the whole class and you can elicit from students why certain answers are right or wrong. When discussing results in class it is very important to be positive and concentrate on what students achieved, rather than on what they got wrong. It is also important not to make students say their own results in public, to avoid highlighting failure and encouraging competition. Another alternative is for students to hand in tasks for you to look at after the class.

In addition to this kind of correction, it can be very useful to establish listening and reading records, which can complement the students' learner diaries. A simple way of doing this is to give students a table or graph, where they assess what proportion of a text they understood each time they read or listened to it. For example, the first time they may understand *20%* of a text (I could understand what it was about more or less). The second time they may understand *50%* (I understood the situation quite well, but I missed a lot of details). The advantages of these records is that they are easy to fill in and students can keep track of their own performance in listening and reading. At the same time students can also think about how well they completed the task. They can thus be made aware of the fact that to do a task they do not need to understand everything.

Look at the example of a listening/reading record. Listen to something in English yourself and complete it. Then copy the record sheets and try out this activity with your students while doing a listening or reading activity (the descriptions of levels of understanding can be in students' L1 if necessary).

With difficult texts you may find that students only understand *25%* the first time but up to *65%* the second time. However, unless the tasks are too difficult, they should have been able to complete the tasks for both first and second listening.

Use these scales to complete the listening/reading graphs below. At the same time say if you managed to complete the task.

100% = I understood absolutely everything

90% = I understood nearly everything. I only missed a few words.

75% = I understood most of it, but I didn't understand a few sentences.

50% = I understood the situation quite well, though I missed a lot of the details.

35% = I got the general idea, but at times I got a bit lost.

20% = I could understand what it was about more or less.

10% = I understood a few words here or there

0% = I didn't understand a single word

Listening/reading record

Date............... **Kind of listening/reading:**...............................

First time	Second time

%
100
90
75
50
35
20
10
0

Task completed: yes/no   **Task completed: yes/no**

Writing

It is difficult to assess one's own written production; therefore students do need correction and assessment of their work by the teacher. However, this is not enough. As mentioned earlier, when teachers give back corrected and assessed work, students often just look at the mark and ignore the rest. Thus a lot of work on the teacher's part is wasted. If learners are to improve their own writing they need to think about their own performance and then compare their judgement with that of the teacher. They also need to try to correct their own mistakes and to think about them, so that in future they will be able to avoid them.

It is useful to do learner training activities that make students aware of the various stages in the writing process. It is particularly important for students to realise the need to check and assess their own work when they have produced a draft. If there is time they can then go on to write a final and corrected draft. One way of developing your students' ability to assess themselves is by getting them firstly to assess texts and then to edit them. In this way they are made aware of some of the criteria involved in assessment. When you do writing activities in class, the first thing to do is to establish clear criteria for assessment before students have started to do a task. Depending on the level and the kind of writing task, criteria could include the following:

- interest and relevance of content
- appropriacy of style
- presentation
- organisation of ideas
- linking and punctuation
- grammatical accuracy and punctuation

An alternative, which can be particularly useful for project work, is to negotiate criteria with students. You can ask students how they think the project should be marked and then work out a simple marking scheme on the board. This activity provides the vital function of making students aware of what constitutes a successful piece of writing. It also involves students in the assessment process.

The next step is to make sure that when students have finished a draft of their work, they check over it, try to correct any simple mistakes they have made and assess the strengths and weaknesses of the writing. It can be a good idea to make students show you an edited version of a first draft before they go on to the final draft. At this stage, peer assessment of work is also very useful. Students can pass their compositions to their partners, who check through it for mistakes and assess it. In the case of group writing, students can check the writing done by other groups. Having produced a final version you can also ask students to make a final assessment of their work, assigning a mark according to the criteria agreed at the beginning. Once again, other students can assess the work and give a mark. This can be done by displaying work around the classroom or by passing the pieces of writing around the class. At first students find this difficult and most tend to give other students high marks, as they do not think that it is up to them to criticise their classmates and friends. However, having done self and peer assessment for a while, marks tend to be more realistic.

The next stage is assessment by the teacher according to the agreed criteria. The teacher's mark is then added to those of the writer and of other students. At the same time the teacher should provide feedback about the problem areas in the compositions. The best way of doing this is through the use of correction codes.

When the compositions are given back to students see if they agree with your assessment. If they can argue coherently that they deserve more marks for one of the factors considered and you feel that they are justified, you can change the mark. In the case of group work, the marks can be discussed with the whole class. You can explain why you gave the mark you did and alter it if the students give convincing reasons. While this process should not degenerate into a bargaining about marks, it is important to take students' opinions into consideration and to show them that 'the teacher is not always right'. This may seem to undermine the teacher's authority, but this is only the case if it is not part of a general approach.

Look at these procedures for carrying out self assessment of writing (described in the preceding paragraphs). Try out one or more stages with a class. While some of the stages are best suited to higher level learners (eg negotiating criteria), other stages (like stage 2- checking and editing) can be done with low level students.

Stage 1: Negotiating criteria (especially good for projects)
Before beginning a writing activity, outline or negotiate criteria for assessing finished work. Write the criteria on the board. One or a combination of these criteria can be used:
- presentation
  handwriting/drawings etc
- content/message
  interesting/relevant to situation
- organisation
  format/paragraphs/organisation of ideas
- linking
  use of linking words and expressions/punctuation
- vocabulary
  adequacy of vocabulary for purpose
- accuracy
  grammatical inaccuracies/spelling/vocabulary

Decide how many points to be given for each area:
Example:
content /10   accuracy /10

Stage 2: Checking and editing
When students have finished writing their first draft, tell them to show it to you. Then they check it for mistakes and give it to their partner to edit.
Stage 3: Final self-assessment
When they have finished the final draft, ask students to assess their own work according to the established criteria.
Stage 4: Final peer-assessment
Display written work around the classroom. Students circulate and write their assessments of each other's work on forms or pieces of paper provided. At the same time, go around yourself and assess work, using the same criteria.
Stage 5: Comparing assessments (better for group writing)
Choose a few pieces of work and compare the different assessments. Discuss differences. Don't be afraid to modify your assessment if students give convincing arguments in favour of a different mark.

Speaking

Speaking is another area where it is very difficult to assess one's own performance. However, a similar approach can be taken as for writing. As this cannot be done for every speaking activity that students do in class, it is best to focus on activities where performance is an important element, for example roleplay or simulation rather than survey activities (where the information is more important). It is also advisable to focus on group or pair performance rather than on individual performance, where peer assessment is involved. Criticism of individual performance (however positive) can be very damaging if it comes from fellow classmates.

As for writing, it is important to establish criteria for assessment before students begin the task: fluency and lack of hesitation, relevance and interest of the performance, pronunciation: sounds/rhythm/word and sentence stress/intonation, appropriacy of language, grammatical accuracy and use of suitable vocabulary. At lower levels students can be encouraged to think about only one or two of these criteria, in particular interest of performance and grammatical accuracy. At higher levels all of these elements need to be considered at one stage or another.

Perhaps before you get students to think about criteria for assessing themselves, it is useful to make them aware of them in general terms. The following learner training activity helps students to think about what is involved in successful communication. It also gives them models for oral self-assessment.

Oral self-assessment

Do this activity yourself. Then try it out with your students.

a Look at the two self-assessments below, with two people assessing how well they performed in an oral exam (a shopping roleplay). Which of them do you think did best in the oral interview?

b Which of these areas do they mention in their self-assessments?
- pronunciation
- grammatical mistakes
- vocabulary
- fluency and hesitation
- getting the message across
- using the appropriate language (in terms of formality) for the situation

A '*I made very few grammatical mistakes, but I spoke very slowly. Sometimes I couldn't think of the word and had to stop completely. My pronunciation was not too bad, but the other person did not understand one or two words and I had to repeat them. I only bought three of the six things I wanted to get.*'

B '*I made a lot of grammatical mistakes, but the 'shop assistant' was able to understand me. I think my pronunciation was not very good and some words were wrong. I spoke at normal speed and when I couldn't think of a word in English I described what it was. I bought what I wanted.*'

Check your answers on page 88.

An important point about self-assessment of speaking is that rather than asking students to give themselves marks, the main thing is for students to think about their problems and their achievements.

Peer assessment should be done during the activity, so that students performing the activity get feedback immediately afterwards. This can either be done in groups or with the whole class. For example, in groups of four, two students can act out roleplays which they have previously practised. The other pair can then give them feedback about their performance. When students act out roleplays or simulations in groups, they can then act them out in front of the class and the other students can assess the overall performance of the group.

Self-assessment of performance can be done immediately after an activity has finished. Students can assess how they performed, either in very general terms or in terms of fluency, accuracy, pronunciation etc. Audio and video taping is of particular use here, as students can go back and see or listen to their own performance. These recordings can also be used to compare performance at different stages of the course, giving students concrete evidence of their progress in speaking.

It is important to complement self-assessment of speaking with your own observation and feedback, pointing out problem areas and encouraging students on what they have achieved. Assessment can also be linked with learner training activities. Having assessed performance in an activity, strategies for improving communication can then be discussed, eg avoiding words that they do not know, using gesture and mime, using words and expressions to hesitate.

3.4 Reviewing progress

In addition to building self-assessment activities into everyday classroom practice, it is important for students to look back and review their own progress over a period of time. This is when self-assessment can be systematically integrated into an overall assessment programme, and linked to the assessment done by the teacher.

However, reviewing one's progress is not an easy task. If students are asked to assess their progress over the past year, without any training or preparation, it is unlikely that they will be able to do it very well. Therefore, reviewing progress needs to be a gradual and cumulative process, building up to a final, global assessment of progress over a course.

A practical model for carrying out self-assessment is suggested:

4 Students use their answers to the end of term questionnaire to make final conclusions

3 Students use their progress reports to assess the term's progress

2 At periodic intervals, students review their own progress

1 Students keep records of what happens in class and how they are doing

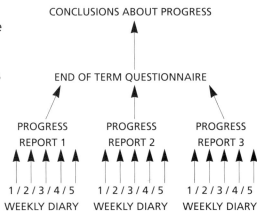

CONCLUSIONS ABOUT PROGRESS

END OF TERM QUESTIONNAIRE

PROGRESS REPORT 1   PROGRESS REPORT 2   PROGRESS REPORT 3

1 / 2 / 3 / 4 / 5   1 / 2 / 3 / 4 / 5   1 / 2 / 3 / 4 / 5
WEEKLY DIARY   WEEKLY DIARY   WEEKLY DIARY

This involves a pyramid approach, where learners use all the records that they have been building up. Firstly, the learner diaries and any other records they may have (eg reading records) can help them complete the periodic progress questionnaires. These questionnaires can be done at the end of a unit or module of a textbook, at the end of a project or coinciding with institutional assessment (when the teacher has to produce some kind of report on students' progress). In turn these progress questionnaires can be used by learners to help themselves assess their progress over a school term or the duration of a course.

Revising

Revising is normally associated with studying for exams, though this does not have to be the case. Revision activities involve going over work done, identifying problems and weaknesses and learning or reinforcing language that has been studied. Thus at this stage, there needs to be an important element of self-assessment, at least if revision is to be efficient.

'Test yourself' or 'self check' activities are one way in which students can check their learning of language and then focus on the problem areas they have. These are now becoming common in textbooks, and are basically tests which students can do and mark themselves. Self check activities normally focus on the grammar studied in a particular unit, but they can also check vocabulary and pronunciation. The formats of these activities are very similar to those used in formal tests. In this way students get practice at doing tasks which they will do in exams. Task types such as editing, gap-filling, multiple choice, word sequencing and classification of lexis can all be used. One fairly simple way of creating these activities is to compile a list of several common mistakes that your students have been making with target structures. Students then have to correct them.

These activities can either be done in class or for homework. It is however useful to go through them with the whole class. In this way you can get an idea of what problems students still have, and what remedial work is necessary. The private nature of these activities is important, as if the teacher collects the results they can become tests. But it is important for them to be done without outside help. If students copy or look at the answers, they are cheating themselves about their own progress. If the activity is done properly, students can use the results from 'self check' activities to help them complete the progress questionnaires.

Self check activity

Look at this activity for beginners. Create a similar activity for your students and give it to them when you have finished a unit or module.

Self check
Do the exercises. Write your total here: /15

1 Correct these sentences:
Example:
My favourite singer are Phil Collins.
My favourite singer is Phil Collins

a I has got two brothers.
b Where you are from?
c What is yours name?

---

d Have got they a television?
e Kangaroos is from Australia.

2 Complete the description with these words:
have
is not
is
are
am
has
have

Example:
My name..is..Emily and I .... from Canada. I ....
got one sister and two brothers. Their names .... Edith, Sam and
Bill. We .... got a dog called Hegel and two cats called Kierke and
Garde. Hegel is a labrador and he .... got black fur. He ....
very intelligent!

3 Look at the family tree. Complete the sentences.
a John is Emily's ....
b Susan is her.............
c Bill is her............
d Tom is her.............

Fred — Anne

John — Susan   Tom

Emily   Sam   Bill

Other revision activities with a self-assessment component involve students looking back at their work and identifying problem areas. For example, students can look through their written work and identify the five most common mistakes they made. In groups they can then work out which mistakes are most common and report them to the rest of the class. Mistakes can then be written up on the board and all the students have to correct them. With lexis, students can look through their work and identify words they find difficult to remember. Similarly with pronunciation, students can look back and select five words which they have difficulty pronouncing.

Tests

As well as comparing marks from formal assessment with students' own assessment of their progress over a period of time, it is important to include an element of self-assessment when giving feedback about tests. This can be done by giving students questionnaires to complete, in order to make them think about their performance in the test. This can also give you useful feedback about your own test.

Look at these test follow-up questionnaires. Adapt them and then try them out with your students after administering a test. Alternatively, think of a test follow-up activity for a different kind of test, eg grammar/vocabulary.

Test follow-up Reading/listening

- How many questions did you get right?
- If you had problems, which of these did you have?
a you had not seen or heard anything like this before
b there was a lot of difficult vocabulary
c (for listening) they spoke too quickly
d (for listening) the sound quality was bad
e the questions were confusing

- Why did you get the questions wrong?
a you did not understand the whole text
b you did not understand a word
c you did not understand a structure
d you answered a question without thinking
e you did not have enough time to answer a question
f you did not understand the instructions

- Do you think the result reflects your level?
- What can you do to improve your listening/reading in the future?

As well as getting students to assess their performance in tests, you can get students to write the tests themselves, especially tests of grammar and vocabulary. Not only is this a good revision activity for students, but it makes them aware of different test formats. This can be done in groups, with one group writing a test for another group. Student-generated tests can also be used in formal assessment in the following way. First, give students a list of the kind of tasks they can use (eg gap-filling/word sequencing). Then, individually or in pairs students write their test and answer sheet. Having collected in all the tests, you can select the best items and write them up on the board. This is the test, which is then administered and marked as any other test. The advantage of this activity is that students feel much more identified with the assessment process. And while one might expect students to write very easy items, this does not happen. In fact the opposite tends to be the case.

Progress questionnaires

Progress questionnaires give learners an opportunity to review their learning over the past few weeks or months. To be able to do this they should use their learner diaries and their listening and reading records. They can also look through their written work: their compositions, notebook and vocabulary book. They also need to consider their results in 'self check' activities and tests. The progress questionnaire pulls together all these different threads to try to give students a global picture of their own progress.

Like learner diaries, the complexity of such questionnaires can vary enormously, depending on time available as well as students' age.

Look at the progress questionnaires. Which one is most suitable for your students?

Questionnaire 1
Think about your progress this term. Give yourself a mark out of ten for these areas:
- speaking   /10
- listening   /10
- reading   /10
- writing   /10
- pronunciation   /10
- grammar   /10
- vocabulary   /10

Questionnaire 2
Use your learner diary to complete the tables with areas that you have covered this term (see examples). Also look at the textbook and your notebook to help you.
Then grade yourself using the scales provided.

Structures studied	Grade
present continuous	4

5 I have no problems with this structure and I never make mistakes.
4 I only make mistakes occasionally
3 I sometimes have problems using it
2 I don't understand it very well and I make a lot of mistakes
1 I don't understand it at all

Vocabulary area	Grade
food and drink	3

5 I have learnt a lot of words
4 I have learnt quite a few words
3 I have learnt some new words
2 I have learnt a few new words
1 I have not learnt any new words

Speaking activities in class	Grade
asking for tourist information	2

5 I can do this very well, without hesitating and making mistakes
4 I can do this quite well, but I sometimes hesitate and make mistakes
3 I can do this, but I speak slowly and make quite a few mistakes
2 I cannot do this very well: I get stuck and can't think of what to say
1 I cannot do this at all

Writing activities done	Grade
letter to penfriend	6

Grade yourself out of ten. Think about these things:
presentation
• content
• organisation
• punctuation
• grammar
• vocabulary

Reading/listening activities	Grade
reading stories	3

5 I did the task with no problems at all
4 I had a few problems
3 I answered half of the questions correctly
2 I only answered a few of the questions
1 I could not do the task

Grade these things (1-5) related to effort and attitude:

participation in class	
use of English in class	
homework and projects	
working in groups	
planning and working on my own	

Questionnaire 3
- Tick which of these things you can do now (✔).
- Put two ticks if you can do it very well (✔✔)
- Put a cross if you can't do it (✗)

a I can talk about what I did yesterday.
b I can ask other people about what they did yesterday.
c I can write about what I did yesterday.
d I can give and ask for directions.
e I can understand simple directions.
f I can write simple directions.
g I can talk about how I get to and from school.
h I can understand a description of a place.
i I can write a description about a place.
j I can describe places.

When your students have finished progress questionnaires you can look at them yourself. If they cover the period of a school term you can link them in with termly assessment. If not, they should be kept along with learners' other records until they can be used for global assessment of progress.

3.5 Results from self-assessment

Having looked at ways of carrying out self-assessment, we need to think about how we can use the results from it and how our students' assessment of themselves can be linked in with our assessment of them. This can be done initially when students complete the periodic progress questionnaires. By collecting these in and looking at them, we can find out how students feel about their own progress and compare them with our own results. If there is a big difference between the two there is obviously a problem, which needs to be sorted out by talking to the student in question.

However, the logical time to link self-assessment with teacher assessment is at the end of a term or course. Students can use the progress questionnaires and other records to make a global assessment of their own progress. This should run parallel to the assessment you do as a teacher. If possible, learners should use the same report or mark sheet that you use. In this way the report done by the student can be directly compared with a draft of the teacher's report.

If there is time, a counselling session can enable you and students to discuss and compare the two global assessments. Firstly, the comments on the student's final report can be negotiated. Secondly, it is possible to discuss the marks. The student's marks from teacher assessment can be compared with his/her own self-assessment. In most cases you will find that student marks will be the same as yours or even lower. When their marks are higher than yours you can ask students to say why they think this is the case. It is possible for students to give convincing reasons for this:, eg *'I did very badly on one of the tests because I was very nervous, but I don't think the mark reflects my real level.'* On such occasions it can be worthwhile modifying his/her mark upwards.

It is very important that these counselling sessions do not degenerate into bargaining sessions about marks. When a student has no reasons to support his/her arguments for a higher mark, the mark should stay the same. But a certain amount of flexibility enables students to feel that their self-assessment is taken seriously and that they are being involved in the assessment process. In the great majority of cases students respond to this by being honest about their progress.

Look at the following procedures for linking end of term/course self-assessment with your own assessment. Would you do it in the same way or would you change anything?

Work out a form to put students marks and your own comments on (comments can be in students' L1). Then complete it for each student.
Example:
Name Ana Gomez García
Listening 7
Speaking 5
Reading 8
Writing 7
Grammar 5
Comments
Ana has worked well this year, especially since Christmas. She still lacks confidence in speaking but she has a good level of understanding. She is still weak in some grammar areas and she needs to revise them thoroughly. However, her compositions have improved and her stories have been excellent and very imaginative. A good year's work!

Give blank copies of the form to your students. Tell them to use their progress reviews to fill it in. Ask them to write at least a sentence about their progress and what they should do to improve next course.

Give the class some puzzles, word games or other activities where they can work on their own. Then call out students one by one. Briefly compare the two reports (yours and the student's). Decide on the final marks and comments. Don't be afraid to change your mark if you feel the student is right.

Time is always a problem, but counselling can be done in the last few days of term after all formal tests have been given and when there is no pressure to cover course material. Activities such as puzzles or reading can enable you to call students to the front of the class while the others are getting on with work on their own.

When a student has a very different mark from yours, it is probably a clear sign that he/she is unable to assess his/her own progress. This may be due to a lack of maturity in outlook or to a real inability to measure progress. In both cases the inability to carry out self-assessment provides clear evidence of problems of attitude. Thus, self-assessment itself provides you as a teacher with important data for assessing non-linguistic factors.

Counselling as mentioned here before can obviously be very time consuming. However, it can be done while students are doing some other activity like reading or doing a project in groups. If at all possible all students should have some kind of direct contact with the teacher, even if it is very brief. This can be either done in the students' L1 or in English where a student's level permits.

In conclusion, this systematic approach to self-assessment builds up to a direct participation of students in the assessment process. As well as providing valuable data for the student, it develops the skill of self-assessment which is not only valuable in language learning. The ability to carry out self-assessment should be a broad educational objective at secondary level.

Suggested answers oral self-assessment

a The second person did much better as he/she was much more fluent and achieved communication, even though he/she made more mistakes.
b Both of them mention all of the things except for appropriacy of language.

Action points: self-assessment

◆ As a result of reading this chapter are you going to implement any of the ideas about self-assessment suggested here? Why/why not?
◆ If you are going to introduce self-assessment with your students, when are you going to do it?
   a at the start of a course
   b during normal classroom activities
   c when you are revising or reviewing a unit or module of your course
◆ Which self-assessment activities are you going to try out?
   Example:
   learner diaries
◆ Are you going to link self-assessment with any other learner training activities?
   Example:
   discussing reading strategies
◆ Are you going to take students' self-assessment into consideration when working out your own final assessment? If so, how are you going to do this?
◆ Are you going to take into account the views that your students' express during self-assessment activities? (For example, in terms of learning preferences, activities, materials etc)

Glossary of terms used in the handbook

accountability
the responsibility we have as teachers to be able to explain the rationale behind our assessment techniques and results to students, parents and institutions

administer tests
the complete process of giving a test including giving out and collection of papers and invigilating or conducting an oral interview

analytic rating scale
scale for rating performance or progress in which different activities are divided into constituent parts and a different band is produced for each activity

assessment
measuring our students' performance in any one of many different ways, diagnosing the problems and measuring the progress students make

band scale
level of performance in a rating scale which describes what a student has achieved in a test

competence
level of performance in the language which our students are actually capable of

correction code
code often used by teachers to signal student errors in written work

counselling
individual meetings between students and teachers to discuss assessment results usually in relation to self-assessment

criterion/criteria
descriptions of what our students should be able to do with the language

criterion-referencing
using descriptions of what our students should be able to do with the language in order to determine the pass score in a test or informal assessment

descriptor
definition of a level of performance in a band scale

diagnostic questionnaires
learner questionnaire used to find out what are our students' problem areas with the language; usually given at the beginning of a course

diagnostic test
type of test used to find out what are our students' problem areas with the language; many progress tests have a diagnostic element

discrete item test format
test format in which there are usually many items requiring short answers

editing
checking our students' written work and correcting mistakes

entry/placement test
test which will indicate at which level a learner will learn most effectively in the case of different levels or streams

evaluation
consideration of all the factors that influence the learning process such as syllabus objectives, course design, materials, methodology, teachers and assessment

examination
formal summative or proficiency test usually administered by an institution; often associated with tests supplied by examination boards

formal assessment
tests given under conditions which ensure the assessment of individual performance in any given area

format
test formats are the tasks and activities which students are required to do (eg multiple choice)

formative assessment
type of assessment which feeds back into learning and gives the learner information on his/her progress throughout a course thus helping him/her to be a more efficient learner

grade
way of expressing overall results using a number or letter

holistic rating scale
scale in which different activities are included over several bands to produce a multi-activity scale

impression mark
number or letter given by a teacher to students' work as a result of informal observation without using a rating scale

informal assessment
system for observation and collection of data about students' performance under normal classroom conditions

integrative test format
type of test format which involves the use of more than one skill by students and which is open-ended involving communication and interaction

inter-rater reliability
way of describing to what extent different raters or teachers assess performance in a test in the same way

interlocutor
teacher or other trained person who during a test acts as the person with whom the student or candidate interacts in order to complete a speaking task

intra-rater reliability
way of describing to what extent the same rater or teacher assesses performance in a test in the same way

item
individual question in a test which requires the student or candidate to produce an answer

learner training
ways of helping learners to find strategies to learn more effectively; these strategies should suit their individual learning style

learner diary
record of students' learning experiences containing what they have done in class, the progress they have made and any problems they have

learning strategies
ways of organising learning which help students to learn more effectively

learning styles/preferences
different ways of learning which learners employ to achieve their objectives

linguistic factors
aspects affecting assessment which are strictly to do with the language such as the four skills

lockstep
situation in which all students in a class are engaged in the same activity at the same time, all progressing through a task at the same rate

monitoring
observing and making of assessments of what is happening in the classroom during learning activities

negotiated syllabus
students' needs and learning preferences are taken into account during a course; these needs will have been discussed by teachers and students together

non-linguistic factors
aspects affecting assessment which are not to do with language per se but are more connected to other factors such as attitude, working within groups and co-operation

norm-referencing
listing students in order of test results and passing them or failing them according to their position on the list

objective marking
where only one answer is possible and this is given in an answer key; possible to be interpreted by all markers

open-ended test format
test format that requires no specific response, but which is open to interpretation

paralinguistic
aspects of communication which are outside the scope of the spoken word such as gestures or expressions

peer assessment
where students assess one another during class activities

peer editing
where checking of students' written work and correction of mistakes is carried out by other students

peer monitoring
where observation and assessments of what is happening in the classroom during learning activities is carried out for students by their class colleagues

performance
how our students did in a formal or informal assessment procedure regardless of their actual competence; performance may be lower than competence

practicality
all aspects concerning tests which affect time and resources

proficiency tests
type of test which aims to describe what a student is capable of doing in a foreign language; usually supplied by external examination boards

profile
written description of students' performance or progress; often used in reporting assessment results

progress questionnaire
learner questionnaire in which students reflect on their own progress over a given period of study

progress tests
type of test which aims to find out how well students have grasped the learning objectives over a particular period of time such as a month, a term or a year or over a number of course modules

rating criteria
the aspects of performance in language or non-linguistic factors on which teachers wish to assess their students

rating
assessing student performance using pre-established scales; usually assessing spoken performance

raw score
number of correct answers obtained by a student in a test; from this score the final grade is often calculated

reliability
the consistency of any form of assessment which means that under the same conditions and with the same student performance the assessment procedure would produce the same results

report
document which describes students' progress and performance

reporting
the process of communicating assessment results to students, their parents and the institution; usually through written reports

rubric
instructions in a test or any classroom activity which indicate to the candidate or student what he/she has to do to complete any given task

sample
the amount of language and content from syllabus plans or teaching records which a test or any classroom activity elicits

scanning
reading a test quickly in order to obtain specific information

self-assessment
assessment carried out by students themselves designed to measure their own performance and progress

self-check activity
where students check their own performance by completing an exercise and then looking at their own results

self-editing
where on completion of a written piece of work, students go through the piece and check themselves for any mistakes

self-monitoring
where students correct their own speech production either at the time of speaking or when listening to a recorded sample of their performance

skimming
reading a text quickly in order to obtain a general idea of the content area

standardisation
agreement between raters of student performance on the meaning and interpretation of criteria used for assessment

subjective marking
where the mark or grade given to a performance depends on somebody's opinion or judgement such as in all speaking tests

summative assessment
type of assessment which aims to measure students' performance at the end of a period of study

summative test
type of test usually administered at the end of courses; often used as a way of deciding whether students move to a higher level or not or obtain a particular certificate or not

test format
description of the task type which is used to elicit any given language sample from candidates and students

test type
overall description of a test in terms of the purpose it serves and its objectivity or subjectivity

test
any form of formal assessment in any language area which is administered under conditions which ensure measurement of individual performance in any given area

validity
where a form of assessment effectively measures what it intends to measure and not something different

washback effect
the influence of tests or examinations on the teaching and learning leading up to the assessment

weighting
the relative importance of different skills and language which is assigned in the assessment process

BIBLIOGRAPHY

Baker, D. *Language Testing: A Critical Survey and Practical Guide* (1989). UK: Edward Arnold.

Black, H.B. & W.B. Dockrell, *Diagnostic Assessment in Secondary Schools. A Teacher's Handbook* (1980). Edinburgh: Scottish Council for Research in Education.

Brindley, G. *Assessing Achievement in the Learner-centred Curriculum* (1989). Sydney: National Centre for English Language Teaching and Research.

Carroll, B.J. *Testing Communicative Performance* (1980). UK: Pergamon.

Carroll, B.J & P.J. Hall, *Make your own language tests: a practical guide to writing language performance tests*. (1985). Oxford: Pergamon.

Davies, A. *Principles of Language Testing* (1990). UK: Blackwell.

Heaton, J.B. *Writing English Language Tests* (1988). UK: Longman.

Heckhausen, N. *The Anatomy of Achievement Motivation* (1967). New York: Academic Press.

Hughes, A. *Testing for Language Teachers* (1989). Cambridge: CUP.

Nunan, D. *The Learner-centred Curriculum* (1988). Cambridge: CUP.

Oller, J.W. Jr. *Language Tests at School* (1979). UK: Longman.

Oskarsson, M. *Approaches to Self-assessment in Foreign Language Learning* (1978). Oxford: Pergamon Press.

Oskarsson, M. Subjective and objective assessment of foreign language performance, (1981) in Read, J.A.S. (ed.) 1981: 225-39.

Read, J.A.S. (ed.). Directions in language testing (1981). SEAMEO Regional Language Centre, Anthology Series 9.

Sumner, R. *The Role of Testing in Schools* (1987). UK: NFER-Nelson.

Weir, C.J. *Communicative Language Testing* (1990). USA: Prentice-Hall.